Also by CHARLES JOHNSON

FICTION

Night Hawks: Stories

Dr. King's Refrigerator and Other Bedtime Stories

Soulcatcher and Other Stories

Dreamer

Middle Passage

The Sorcerer's Apprentice

Oxherding Tale

Faith and the Good Thing

NONFICTION

The Way of the Writer: Reflections on the Art and Craft of Storytelling

The Words and Wisdom of Charles Johnson

Taming the Ox: Buddhist Stories and Reflections on Politics, Race, Culture, and Spiritual Practice

Passing the Three Gates: Interviews with Charles Johnson
(edited by Jim McWilliams)

Turning the Wheel: Essays on Buddhism and Writing

King: The Photobiography of Martin Luther King Jr.
(with Bob Adelman)

I Call Myself an Artist: Writings by and about Charles Johnson
(edited by Rudolph P. Byrd)

Africans in America: America's Journey through Slavery
(with Patricia Smith)

Black Men Speaking
(with John McCluskey Jr.)

PHILOSOPHY

Philosophy: An Innovative Introduction: Fictive Narrative, Primary Texts, and Responsive Writing
(with Michael Boylan)

Being and Race: Black Writing Since 1970

DRAWINGS

Half-Past Nation Time

Black Humor

CHILDREN'S FICTION

The Adventures of Emery Jones, Boy Science Wonder: The Hard Problem
(with Elisheba Johnson)

The Adventures of Emery Jones, Boy Science Wonder: Bending Time
(with Elisheba Johnson)

The Adventures of Emery Jones, Boy Science Wonder: The Tomorrow No One Wanted
(with Elisheba Johnson)

Charles Johnson

GRAND

A Grandparent's Wisdom
for a Happy Life

A Work from the Johnson Construction Co.

HANOVER
SQUARE
PRESS

**HANOVER
SQUARE
PRESS™**

Recycling programs
for this product may
not exist in your area.

ISBN-13: 978-1-335-01586-0

Grand: A Grandparent's Wisdom for a Happy Life

This edition published by arrangement with Harlequin Books S.A.

Library of Congress Cataloging-in-Publication Data has been applied for.

Hanover Square Press
22 Adelaide St. West, 40th Floor
Toronto, Ontario M5H 4E3, Canada
HanoverSqPress.com
BookClubbish.com

Printed in U.S.A.

For my grandson, Emery Charles Spearman.

CONTENTS

INTRODUCTION

Where there is no vision, the people perish.

Proverbs 29:18

O nce upon a time the cluttered study where I've written books of all kinds for twenty-six years, and drawn all manner of cartoons and illustrations, was all my own. When I remodeled our house in 1992, the room was designed by two architects to be my office, with floor-to-ceiling bookshelves for literature and philosophy, a drawing table with a glass top, and an L-shaped counter on which to place my PC, office equipment, little Bud-

dhist statues and a Tibetan prayer wheel, figurines of famous writers and thinkers (Twain, Poe, Martin Luther
King Jr., Bodhidharma), and grown-up toys to delight
an old sci-fi and comic book fanboy like me—the space-
ship from *When Worlds Collide* and a miniature Stargate.
This was my workspace, a room that externalized my
own mind and creative spirit. Just sitting there in the
comfortable leather chair at my scarred and worn school-
house desk, or on my meditation cushion (zafu) was all
I needed each day to be inspired.

But eight years ago, my grandson Emery was born.
And apparently this room inspires him, too, because he
now calls it *his* office.

I watch in wonder as he, a beautiful and brilliant boy
who feels at home in a room of books and artistic tools,
takes over my workspace for his projects. He raids my
ream of paper on a bookshelf for his own drawings and
books. He creates origami objects—houses, airplanes,
pouches—because his imagination seems inexhaustible.
An only child, as I was, he listens intensely to the ways
adults talk, and tries out our grown-up language just
to see how it rolls off his tongue. But he knows more
than English since he's in his second year at the French
American School of Puget Sound and speaks French
better than I ever will. (The ninth-century king Char-
lemagne would love this school's curriculum, having

once concluded that "to know another language is to have a second soul.") There, at that school, his weekly schedule is heavy on classes for science and coding, a skill that when he grows up will be as necessary as typing was for my generation. Added to which, he's been able to read since he was in preschool, so I'm forever asking him *not* to read over my shoulder as I type personal emails to friends. I know his grandmother deserves the credit for his early reading ability because she was once an elementary school teacher and taught him as well as our son and daughter to read. And his mother, Elisheba, a conceptual artist and poet, should be credited for stimulating his imagination by reading him a story every night since the day he was born. Furthermore, he knows that the main character in the middle grade series of books I coauthor with his mother, *The Adventures of Emery Jones, Boy Science Wonder*, is named after him. He tells me what he thinks should happen to Emery Jones in the books to come—and draws for me his version of the characters in the first three books in the series.

So, yes, he is a constant source of wonder for me. He takes guitar lessons and tap dancing and loves to demonstrate the latter. Also his skill at break dancing. He *is* a natural show-off, very self-confident, and sometimes I've caught him watching his own reflection in the sliding glass door that leads from my study to a deck outside, reveling in his own little, brown, dreadlocked image, knowing how handsome he is—especially when his big smile lights up the room—as he sits on my desk and tells me a story about his friends. Perhaps someday he'll try out acting; in a few days he will be one of the leads in his summer camp's production of *The Lion King*. One of my dear friends calls him my mini-me, but I know that when I was his age, I was never as confident and self-assured as this kid growing up in a home of very educated, creative people.

On the contrary, my hardworking father only went as far as the fifth grade. In 1920s South Carolina, his own father insisted that the six boys in the family leave school to help him on his farm (the six girls, my aunts, were allowed to stay in school). And my mother? She was a housewife with a high school education, but she loved reading and art, was in three book clubs, and of course her influence on me was huge. Nevertheless, mine was a blue-collar, working-class background—summer jobs hauling garbage in sweltering heat at nineteen when I first began to train in Asian martial arts; and before that when I was in high school a holiday job working the night shift until dawn on at a conveyor belt at a Rand McNally Co. in Skokie, Illinois, slapping glue on *Physician's Desk Reference* books.

My father taught me not to be afraid of work. In my early teens, he was the one black man I saw day and night, the closest example I had for measuring my own strengths and weaknesses. He became my first meditation on manhood. My challenge. My Rosetta stone. When there was something he felt he needed to do, he was focused like a dog chewing a bone until it was done. I would sometimes study him, waiting for him to slip, which he never did, even though in the late 1950s a black criminal stole every penny he'd saved to buy our first home. (No need to elaborate on this, except to say that I watched my father lean against the doorway of the apartment where we lived, smoking his ubiquitous cigar, silent as a tree, and staring—just staring—off into space, reviewing his options after this disaster, figuring out how to make his next move.) After that loss, I watched him work three jobs in the early 1960s to support my mother and me—a day job doing construction, an evening job as a night watchman, and on the weekends he logged hours helping an elderly white couple fix up their house in a North Shore suburb—a couple that remained friends of our family until their deaths. Around our house Dad was never idle, nor did he let me do much woolgathering. If he wasn't painting the house, he was repairing something; if he wasn't repairing something, he was planning some improvement he intended to make (and whenever he came to visit *my* home in Seattle, he was forever tinkering with things I'd been too busy to attend).

For decades he was content to own but one carefully preserved suit, which he wore to Ebenezer AME Church. He loved to hear the minister preach and the choir sing. Despite his workaholic habits, he told his white employers that he would do overtime and time and a half on holidays, but he would never, never work on a Sunday because, as he put it, "Sunday is for church." He was always in bed by 11:00 p.m., and up precisely at 6:30 in the morning, even during his years of retirement. A proud, quietly pious man, he paid for my college education, expecting me to acquire the professional diploma that circumstances had prevented him from getting.

And he taught me, I truly believe, *how* to work—indeed, to see whatever I did, regardless of how humble the labor, as being a portrait of myself. And never to stop until my goal was realized. To disappoint him or my mother—that I dreaded, as a boy, more than anything on earth. I cannot doubt that he learned what he knew about duty from *his* father, a farmer and a blacksmith. Or that in an earlier era of black American history, his deep sense of responsibility, Protestant work ethic, and pride were widely shared by black American men. Of course, he experienced racism— my relatives in the South have ample horror stories to tell, but when I was young and eagerly probed them for every gory detail, perversely hoping to hear their personal stories about the Klan, lynchings, and the inexhaustible dirty deeds of white people, my aunts and uncles simply shook their heads and said, "It's better to leave that behind."

One family member who left it behind in order to keep moving forward was my father's uncle, William Johnson, whose biography I invoked often when my son and I talked late into the night about being black men in this country. Our Uncle Will also hailed from rural South Carolina, and a life close to the land. His people farmed, spent their winters hunting, and produced nearly everything they needed. Their water came from a well. Answering nature's call in the middle of the night meant a lonely walk outside to a foul-smelling outhouse, one's feet stepping gingerly to avoid snakes. They put their children to work at age five, making them bring water for the adults and older children as they worked. In their daily lives nothing came easily, nothing was taken for granted, and I am convinced that as a young man in his twenties, Uncle Will imbibed Booker T. Washington's famous program of self-reliance and his "philosophy of the toothbrush."

I remember him as a bald, dark-skinned, potbellied, suspender-wearing family patriarch (a role my father later assumed) who had a pew reserved just for him in our church (he tithed heavily), watched the evening news on his black-and-white TV as if it were the Oracle of Delphi, and loved to see his brother's kids and his great-nephews and great-nieces come over for Thanksgiving and Christmas dinner in the two-story apartment building he had designed and built himself. He lived, naturally, on the top floor, and had his office, with its maps and blueprints that anticipated my own cluttered study today. Towering over every one of us children (and everyone else in our family), he counseled us to "get an education, that's the most important thing you can do—not having one is the only thing that slowed me down."

As he told the story—his own story—when Will Johnson arrived in Evanston during the Depression, he realized that white-owned milk companies did not deliver to black people. So he became, he said, the first black milkman in Evanston, delivering milk for a white milk company. He even came up with a jingle for his business, which he sang to me once, though I've forgotten it now. Later, he worked on a construction crew until he learned the ropes, then started his second business, the Johnson Construction Company, which was responsible for raising churches (Springfield Baptist Church), apartment buildings, and residences all over the North Shore area—places where today, long after my great-uncle's death in 1989 at age ninety-seven, people still live and worship. In fact, once this business took off, he was able to promise jobs for his siblings, nieces, and nephews if they came north. My father accepted his offer and met my mother shortly after relocating to the Chicago area, and that encounter led to me entering this world.

As a child, I remember riding around Evanston with my father. He would point to a building under construction, and say, "Your Uncle Will is building that place." I grew up surrounded by my family's creativity and industry all over my hometown. Today I honor my great-uncle's business by using its name on the title page of all my books.

My son and daughter heard me preach the preceding story often enough for it to have the effect of a sleeping pill. But I repeated it, mantra-like, as much for my benefit as for theirs, and primarily to remind myself that culture and civilization are but one generation deep. Yes, they can be lost in a mere twenty years. The blink of an eye. They are not givens. And if I do not tell the story of their grand- and great-grandelders, my grandson— weaned on the less than responsible media—may never know that even in the face of staggering racial obstacles (beside which today's bigotry pales), our elders in the pre–civil rights era raised strong, resourceful sons and daughters. Their intention—their personal sacrifices and lifelong labor—was to prepare their offspring for the opportunities they themselves were denied.

Naturally, I love watching Emery in the present. But I sometimes worry about his future. What will his world be like as he grows into adolescence, then young manhood? Do I have any "wisdom," based on my seventy-one years of experience, worth sharing with him? Are there any perennial truths that I—as a writer, artist, academically trained philosopher, Buddhist practitioner, martial artist and former journalist and college professor—can impart to Emery that might make his journey through life easier or more rewarding?

Looking at the problems I see in the world around me, I realize there are so many things I want to say to him about the goodness, truth, and beauty that life offers. And I want to warn him about the dangers, too, all the minefields I hope he'll avoid in order to know happiness and prevent unnecessary suffering. A part of me is hesitant to do that. One problem is that grandfatherly advice is as plentiful as blackberries.

Another problem is that the world of my experiences is in so many ways vastly different from the one Emery will live through. I was born shortly after World War II and was exactly his age when the civil rights movement began in Montgomery, Alabama, when Rosa Parks refused to relinquish her seat on a segregated bus to a white man. The next decade would see an end to the legal racial segregation that caused my parents and ancestors such suffering and grief. Then as the second half of the twentieth century unfurled, I witnessed America's emergence as a superpower, the Cold War, the Space Race, the slow but steady emergence of a counterculture among my peers in the 1960s, a women's liberation movement establishing itself by the 1970s, this nation's first unwinnable war in Vietnam, the gradual transformation of America's two dominant political parties and a growing distrust of politics after Watergate, the invention of the internet, the expansion of colleges and universities after World War II (and every graduating student today realizing he or she will change careers and/or jobs at least five times during their lives), the fading away of the older economy my father knew and the rise of a global economy dominated by STEM skills, same sex marriage and the legalization of marijuana, shootings in our public schools, the global damage caused by climate change, ongoing and seemingly intractable conflicts in the Middle East, cloning and the creation of chimeras, human missions to Mars, and many more differences between the world of his grandparents and the world he may experience.

A third problem is that we believe in sharing our wisdom with younger generations. But from a Buddhist perspective is this really possible? "Wisdom" is fixed, codified, static. The world, on the other hand, is constantly changing. Inevitably, the "wisdom" we impart is about the past, an impermanent state of affairs that may no longer apply to the "now."

I don't expect Emery to one day embrace Buddhism, or to become a philosopher. But I do want him to think. If he is always in an interrogative frame of mind, always questioning, always wondering, "Why?" he will see that at any moment in the history of culture there is more non-sense than sense. He will realize that it is every serious thinker's job to sustain the frail light of clarity and reason in the ever-present darkness of ignorance, superstition, ideology, dogma, prejudice, and demagoguery.

And so I wonder if there is something—*any*thing— that a member of my often-maligned generation can share with his grandchildren? Some things that are timeless or come close to being so?

So it is tentatively, and with great humility that I offer this advice, condensed into what I hope are ten fertile and essential ideas for the art of living to my grandson and those other children in his generation. I offer these words not as rules or absolutes, but instead in the hopeful spirit that led Franklin D. Roosevelt to say, "We cannot always build the future for our youth, but we can build our youth for the future."

Yet I would do wrong if I left you with the impression

that giving helpful advice is a one-sided activity, because at this very moment, the future comes marching into my study, long dreadlocks swinging behind him, some of them obscuring his face until he pushes them away.

I say, "Bonjour, Dr. Emery." (I want him to get it in his head early that one day the titles "Dr." or "PhD" will be something within his reach since less than 3 percent of Americans have earned a doctorate.) "You doin' okay, buddy?"

He replies, *"Oui,"* circles around the chair where I'm sitting, and, holding a fistful of playing cards, climbs on top of my desk.

I ask, "What're those?"

"Pokémon."

Emery explains how the Pokémon game is all the rage among his friends in second grade. I look at the cards, confused by animals named Pikachu, Hariyama, and Raichu. Apparently, they possess different powers. I have to confess that the old cartoonist and comic book geek in me is fascinated by the imaginative world they seem to inhabit. The child in *me* starts to awaken. I love seeing things through his fresh eyes. I remember Oliver Wendell Holmes's insight that "men do not quit playing because they grow old; they grow old because they quit playing."

After cutting the deck of cards into two piles, and

giving me one, Emery explains the Byzantine rules of Pokémon.

Then he says, "Put down a card."

I place a card from the top of my pile in front of him. Then Emery throws down his card. Somehow his card beats mine, which he tosses into a discard pile.

"I lost?"

"Grandpa," he says patiently, "you'll get the hang of this. Trust me. Just keep playing, and I'll help you."

I keep playing, pleased by the realization that in the dialectic of learning between grandparents and grandchildren, in this give-and-take between generations, both sides have something to teach each other.

1

KNOW
THYSELF

This is perhaps the oldest wisdom in the Western world, attributed to the ancient Athenians, and probably the hardest of goals to achieve. (I'll explain why it's so hard in a moment.) During Emery's life, he will encounter many people eager to tell him who—and what—he is. Many will see him through the lens of their own limitations. And, unfortunately, many will not have his best interests in mind. Some might even try to lead him into activities that will damage or make difficult his future.

For that reason, I'll tell him he has to protect his reputation even before he has one.

However, as his grandfather, I will ask him to not judge harshly anyone who directs negativity his way. Everyone he meets in his daily life will be at a different stage of intellectual, moral, and spiritual development. Emery will need to see that as he moves through the seasons of his life from childhood to adolescence, then through adulthood and old age, as he evolves, he himself will be on differing, ever more refined levels of understanding, experience, and maturity as well as moral and spiritual development.

Making matters even more difficult, each individual he meets during the course of his day is, as the great spiritual teacher Eknath Easwaran once pointed out, most likely emerging *from* a state of depression, is already *in* a state of depression, or is about to *enter* a state of depression, and that includes his parents and grandparents. I want Emery to do as I was taught—to "honor thy mother and father." But he will someday recognize how they, too, are human beings who have to negotiate their ways as individuals through this life, perhaps failing or falling short of someone's idea of perfection. He should think of them with gratitude and forgiveness.

He should think of his own life that way as well, never

forgetting, as the saying goes, that "we all have the right to be wrong" sometimes.

But what he should always remember is something I told his mother as she was growing up: namely, there has never been anyone in this world exactly like him. There will never be anyone in this world exactly like him again. (As much as I'd like to claim this thought is original to me, Friedrich Nietzsche beat me to it when he wrote, "At bottom every man knows well enough that he is a unique being, only once on this earth; and by no extraordinary chance will such a marvelous, picturesque piece of diversity in unity as he is ever be put together a second time.") No two people have the same story. This is true of all us and no reason for anyone to get a big head about it, because understanding his uniqueness as well as what he shares with everyone who has ever lived or will live is the task of a lifetime.

"The thing that Americans have to learn over and over again," the great novelist Ralph Ellison once observed, "is that they are individuals and have the responsibility of individual vision." That understanding was shared by another great writer, James Baldwin, when in his essay "The New Lost Generation" he said, "A man is not a man until he's able and willing to accept his own vision of the world, no matter how radically this vision departs from that of others."

As Baldwin suggests, pursuing one's own vision can sometimes be a lonely affair, but if Emery finds himself in such a situation, he might find bracing Judy Garland's advice: "Always be a first-rate version of yourself, and not a second-rate version of someone else."

The injunction to develop one's own vision is related to another idea attributed to the ancient Greeks: *The unexamined life is not worth living.* What does it mean, then, to examine one's life as one is living it? Let me try to unravel this question with a personal anecdote, one I will share with my grandson.

When I was in my teens and early twenties, I was forever testing myself, even beyond the parameters of what my parents and teachers felt I should know or be able to do. Why? Well, I was curious about everything in the world around me. I wanted to acquire, as Thoreau says in *Walden*, "as many skills as fingers on the hand." And perhaps instinctively, as a black American student, I sensed that the curriculum presented to me by my teachers was incomplete. I knew what was missing in the public schools I attended because I knew the stories about black life told to me by my family members, friends, and works of scholarship by authors of color.

In the 1950s and '60s, our schools marginalized or erased completely the history and contributions of people of color. To a certain degree, and down through history, "education" has always contained an element of social and cultural indoctrination. When a society feels it has a problem, it turns to the schools to fix it. It's an honest and sincere effort of teachers—and adults in general—to shape young people in the image of what they think is best, based on their own experience. But the best teachers expect their students to go further than they were able to. How else across generations can progress in culture and civilization be achieved? This is what Isaac Newton meant when he said, "If I have seen further than others, it is by standing on the shoulders of giants." For he understood that "what we know is a drop, what we don't know is an ocean."

Emery should be wary, then, of teachers or adults who profess to know everything, or use their greater knowledge like a weapon. Such a teacher is much like the schoolyard bully Emery has told me about. (I won't mention the kid's name.)

As he grows older, Emery will realize that all my life I've been a teacher, and therefore I've always been acutely aware of how little content one can cover in a ten-week quarter or a semester. In that time, teachers and students can only skim the surface of a subject. So a student must always maintain his or her curiosity and go beyond the parameters of the courses teachers create. Limited classroom time inevitably means most if not all courses are incomplete. They can only provide a foundation.

In seventy-one years I've had to reinvent myself at least three times. I became a professional cartoonist and illustrator in my teens because of my talent and passion for drawing, spending seven years producing comic art that resulted in my 1970 PBS series, *Charlie's Pad*, where I taught cartooning on television. When I was an undergraduate, I and my fellow black students in 1969 contributed as small discussion group leaders to the first black history survey course on the campus of the college we attended. After that, I trained to become a philosopher and earned a PhD in the subject, which I taught when I was a graduate student. And then by necessity I became an English professor and literary scholar, teaching the craft of literary fiction and creative writing. Since the age of nineteen, I have been a martial artist, studying several Asian fighting systems and for ten years teaching the one known as Choy Li Fut kung fu.

So what? Emery might say. So *this* is how I'll respond: We can only "know ourselves," what our capacities and limitations are, as we move through life and the unique challenges it presents to us. And if we are open to change. For that reason, self-examination will be necessary for him at every stage and season of his life, because he is a process, not a product.

That simple fact—our lives being characterized by change—is surely what makes self-examination a challenge every day. But equally interesting is the fact that in the midst of change some things about us remain the same. Obviously, this is not true for our bodies, these vehicles we use to move through the world. But what about Emery's mind and spirit? When he examines them, will he also find they are subject to ceaseless change with nothing stable or permanent?

Let's start by taking a look at the mind.

Many Eastern philosophers have for thousands of years studied the labile, mercurial behavior of our minds. In the canonical Buddhist text, the *Dhammapada*, we find this observation:

Hard to hold down,
nimble,
Alighting wherever it likes:
the mind.
Its taming is good.
The mind well-tamed
Brings ease.

By its very nature, the mind is restless. In *Raja-Yoga*, the nineteenth-century philosopher-teacher Vivekananda employed a popular East Indian metaphor for the mind's contumacy, one found sprinkled throughout Hindu and Buddhist literature:

There was a monkey, restless by its own nature, as all monkeys are. As if that were not enough, someone made him drink freely of wine, so that the monkey became still more restless. A scorpion stung him. When a man is stung by a scorpion, he jumps about for a whole day; so the poor monkey found his condition worse than ever. To complete his misery a demon entered into him. What language can describe the uncontrollable restlessness of that monkey? The human mind is like that monkey, incessantly active by its own nature, then it becomes drunk with the wine of desire, thus increasing its turbulence. After desire takes possession comes the sting of the scorpion of jealousy of the success of others, and last of all the demon of pride enters the mind, making it think itself of all importance. How hard to control such a mind.

Vivekananda's humorous yet horrifyingly recognizable "monkey mind" is, obviously, *unclear*. Such a mind is completely out of control. But there is now a very popular but also ancient skill for examining the mind that someday I will teach Emery. In the Buddhist *Mahasatipatthana Sutta* (Great Mindfulness Discourse), Shakyamuni Buddha advises his disciples to "abide contemplating feelings as feelings...mind as mind...(and) mind-objects as mind-objects."

The simplicity of that advice conceals an entire universe of our conscious experience. In what is known as Vipassana or "insight" meditation, we direct our attention to one of the closest activities to us—the in-and-out flow of our breaths. (Once, when Emery's mother was five or so, she saw me sitting and referred to my practice as "medicating," and in a sense she was right; each meditation session is medicinal.)

Try, if you can, to focus on your breath and nothing else for five minutes. This is no easy task. After a few seconds, the mind will wander from following the breaths to memories, projections for future plans, thoughts, reveries, and to an entire mental panorama. So when the mind begins to wander, we dutifully yet gently bring it back to the in-and-out rhythm of our breathing. We do not scold ourselves for these lapses of attention and focus.

Eventually, the practitioner of Vipassana sees that, like the rising and falling movement of his breath, each thought, emotion, and feeling—anger, say, or pride, jealousy, self-pity, fear, desires of any sort—is impermanent, passing away like clouds moving across the sky if he or she attends to them long enough. Furthermore, the practitioner sees that he or she is not these feelings, these emotions. They simply arise. They can dispassionately be examined or analyzed, and we are always free to let go the negative feelings and thoughts, and to revisit and reinforce those feelings that most benefit ourselves and others, like unselfish love.

This, then, is one way to create an examined life worth living.

Would it be safe to say that over the course of our lives those ideas and feelings we hold on to and nourish are ones that do not change and, therefore, might be called our passions? I would like to think so, yet a sad experience comes to mind that one day I will share with Emery.

On September 12, 2003, I delivered a lecture titled "Storytelling and the Alpha Narrative" for the Field's End literary organization on Bainbridge Island, Washington. During the Q&A, I urged those in attendance to find their passion. Afterward, as I chatted with different people, a gentle, soft-spoken, middle-aged black man approached me. He said, "I've been searching all my life for my passion, and I haven't found it." I was at a loss for how to respond to him. Or what I might say to help him, because a passion for doing something is, at least in my experience, finding something one loves. What we *choose* reveals what we *are*. And in my life I've loved so many things the challenge was also how to bring them all together, unified in a single life.

As I rode the ferry from Bainbridge back to Seattle, this gentleman's situation lingered in my mind. Had he really found nothing to be passionate about? To love unselfishly and desire to serve? As the ferry drew closer to the glittering lights of the city, the moonlight struck the waves, which rose up like individual, flicker-flash human lives—separate and seemingly distinct—and a moment later disappeared back into Puget Sound. My thoughts turned to something said by philosopher William James: "Most people live, whether physically, intellectually or morally, in a very restricted circle of their potential being. They make use of a very small portion of their possible consciousness, and of their soul's resources in general, much like a man who, out of his whole bodily organism, should get into a habit of using and moving only his little finger."

As Emery grows, learning more and more about himself, and examining his life at every turn, I truly hope he will find a lifelong passion—something he loves—the devotion to which brings him happiness. If he does, he will understand a statement made by the great spiritual teacher Eknath Easwaran that I've had taped to my desk since 1981, alongside one from the *Upanishads*:

A well-spent life is one that rounds out what it has begun. The life of a great scientist or artist is usually shaped by a single desire, carried through to the very end.

And he'll grasp the meaning of this from the *Upanishads*:

We are what our deep, driving desire is.
As our deep, driving desire is, so is our will.
As our will is, so is our deed.
As our deed is, so is our destiny.

2

LIFE IS NOT PERSONAL, PERMANENT, OR PERFECT

As he grows up, Emery will learn that we live in the midst of intriguing mysteries. And the greatest of those mysteries is himself.

Among the thousands of books in our house, he might come across one by Insight Meditation teacher Ruth King, titled *Mindful of Race: Transforming Racism from the Inside Out*. It's a book I'll tell him he can trust. Filled with wisdom, King's book differs from most that address the experience of "race" by refocusing our attention on the basis for all our experiences, which is consciousness itself, and she does so with a simple three-part formula that is easy to remember.

In her book, King tells us that "life is not personal, permanent, or perfect." We would be wise, I think, to look at this trifecta of statements one at a time.

First, Emery should ask himself, "What *is* a person?" Are we body? A mind? A self? If his journey through life takes him to David Hume's *Treatise on Human Nature*, as my journey did, he will be asked to consider that philosopher's statement that "for my part, when I enter most intimately into what I call myself, I always stumble on some particular perception or other, of heat or cold, light or shade, love or hatred, pain or pleasure, and can never observe anything but the perception." He grasped the error at the heart of Descartes's famous conclusion in *Meditations on First Philosophy*, "I think, therefore I am." What is the error? Simply that all one can say honestly and empirically is that "thought is going on." The addition of *I* to his conclusion was an unnecessary interpolation.

The reason Hume could not find a "myself" when he looked within is simply because such an enduring entity or "substance" does not exist. To him we are just our consciousness or awareness. We are thoughts without a thinker, verbs and not nouns, through which an infinite number of feelings arise and pass away. However, as he moves through this life many, many people will try to convince my grandson Emery that he is not only a noun but is trapped within someone's definition of the meaning of that noun. For philosopher Alfred North Whitehead this belief in substance is the Fallacy of Misplaced Concreteness. And, tragically, it is a fallacy alive and well in our world every day, causing immeasurable grief and suffering, especially when we judge others based on superficial appearances and their merely cosmetic characteristics.

I know that throughout Emery's life he will be prematurely and superficially judged by others based on, say, his hair, complexion, height, and other cosmetic details about him. That is unavoidable in the social world. However, as his grandfather, one of my duties is to make him aware that while others may foolishly behave this way, he should practice what I call egoless listening, by which I mean he should put aside his ego when others are speaking to him. And remember philosopher Epictetus's amusing thought that "we have two ears and one mouth so that we can listen twice as much as we speak." Without judgment, without interpretations, he should in the presence of others cast off any assumptions or presuppositions he might have about them. He and they are without an essence. Without a fixed meaning. He should just look. And listen to the open-ended, phenomenologi-cal profiles of that person as they unfold before him and understand that he can never know others in the fullness and complexity of their being, just as they cannot know completely the complexities he represents. That means he must always be respectful of others. And if they are not always respectful toward him? Well, he must simply remember that regardless of what others come at him with, and despite how they judge or "interpret" him, there is actually no static, fixed "him" there at all. Even if he lives with someone for fifty years, they will have important, ineffable experiences, thoughts, and feelings unknown to him. Dimensions of their being will neces-sarily be cloaked in mystery. Language (even thought), for all its power and precision, can only skim the surface of that inexhaustible mystery that he and others are. He can never see the world completely from their histori-cally conditioned perspective. Nor will others be able to completely see the world through Emery's eyes or know what is contained in all the chambers of his heart. And so, if he always listens egolessly and mindfully—if he can remember that all our knowledge is provisional—others will always inspire wonder. I want him to experience discovery—learning—as *delicious*. Because he will see—as Walt Whitman saw—that each one of us, and any-thing we examine with patience, contains multitudes.

That realization will ease Emery into the second truth in King's formula. Nothing is, or can be, permanent, including this universe itself. That observation seems simple enough. But if my grandson ponders and probes its implications, he will see that the fact of impermanence leads him inexorably to an ethical position. Whatever is, is just a flicker-flash of beauty against the backdrop of eternity, carrying within itself its own ending. Aware of this, Emery will feel in each moment how ephemeral everything is and, because of that, how precious all sentient beings are. I'm sure he will be amused, as some of my friends are, that I am unable to kill even insects. In our home, I keep a jar to capture them—spiders and moths and mosquitoes in the summer—and then release in my backyard to live out the rest of their brief lives.

"Change" and "impermanence" are simply words we use to describe the fact that everything dies. And most often so that something else may be born. This wisdom is expressed in some Asian cultures where one never allows oneself to feel too high when things are "good" and never to feel too low when we judge our situation to be "bad." Neither situation can stay that way forever.

That being the case, I want my grandson to understand in his bones, in his depths, that when his life's journey hits a rough patch; when he may be broke and hungry with bill collectors at his door; when there seems to be nowhere he can turn for help and every hand seems turned against him; when he feels he must during his life cross a racial minefield seeded with centuries of IEDs by whites, blacks, and others, by those on the left and the right; when he may be misunderstood and suffering in solitude—I want Emery to see that if he can stay the course and ride out the rough patch, what he feels is a "bad" situation must inevitably change. If he hits bottom, there is nowhere to go but up. And if he can weather these stormy periods that come to every life, they will make him stronger and wiser. He will understand what is meant in the saying that "a diamond was once a piece of coal that handled pressure very well."

Just as his circumstances must change during his life, so must Emery understand that he can always change his life to fit new circumstances and reinvent himself. As Ruth King says, "We are a series of ever-changing elemental processes, all arising and passing away. Who we are emerges out of interrelating causes and conditions." Put another way, he will always have personal agency. He will always be free. Especially free, not in what life throws at him, but in how he decides to react to that.

There is a time-honored word for this flexibility in life: jazz.

That unique contribution to American music and culture contains, in theory and practice, the importance of improvisation, i.e., not being locked into a pre-established text, being open to the rich possibilities of the present moment, and understanding that each action is new and unrepeatable in the present moment, the *here* and *now*. A reliable guide for Emery to grasp this principle is Herbie Hancock, who explained improvisation in a 2007 interview for Beliefnet:

> "The cool thing is that jazz is really a wonderful example of the great characteristics of Buddhism... At our best we're nonjudgmental. If we let judgment get in the way of improvising, it always screws us up. *So we take whatever happens and try to make it work*." (Italics mine.)

An awareness of change and impermanence will also temper and refine Emery's experience of "good" times in a way that is healthy. During those times when his desires are fulfilled and he gets whatever it is that he thinks he wants, Emery will, of course, want those moments to continue. The danger is that he will become attached to them, like writers and actors I've known who, after the experience of success and momentary applause, squander decades of their lives struggling to repeat that pleasurable experience. But I hope he will remember a story I'll tell him that appears in Margo McLoughlin's

"In the Sky There Is No Footstep," one of the delightful tales in *Nixon Under the Bodhi Tree and Other Works of Buddhist Fiction*. There we are introduced to a senior monk who has a love of chocolate. To celebrate his birthday, one of his students makes him a delicious cake. "(He) would grin when he saw the cake," the story tells us. "He would take each bite and savor it, but when the cake was gone, he would let it go."

Letting go when the time is right to do so, not clinging to anything that will inevitably change as one is chasing it, might prove to be one of the hardest life lessons that Emery will have to learn. Letting go can be hard. There is a sweet sadness to it. But there need not be the feeling of loss. Only a sense of completion. And freedom. One day we will have to let everything go. You'll never see luggage on a hearse, I'll one day tell my grandson. My takeaway from that little bit of folk wisdom is that in this life we live best when we are devoted to giving, not to accumulating.

In our society, I know Emery will encounter many (and perhaps most) people who don't feel joy at the thought of change and impermanence but instead anxiety, perhaps even fear. For impermanence destroys our desire for certainty. But even our best scientific explanations can only be, as Plato suggests in the *Timaeus*, "a likely story." It isn't that our lack of certainty about what things mean arises from an absence or lack of meaning. Rather, we live with this state of affairs because there is an overabundance of meaning. In a word, things we believe we are familiar with already mean too much and always outstrip our perception. (The simple reason for this is that there are eight billion people—consciousnesses—on this Earth, and each can potentially call forth a new profile, sense, or meaning for a phenomenon.) Emery can also think of this in terms of Ralph Ellison's *Invisible Man*, appreciating how most of what happens in our world (to say nothing of the ever-changing universe) goes unseen, unreported, unrecorded, and remains "invisible." What we know is always vastly outweighed by what we don't know and may never know, and we really do live our lives in the midst of great mysteries.

For that reason, Emery will have to accept Ruth King's advice that perfection is impossible. Also that "shit happens" beyond his control, and that this can be a good thing. In other words, experience will throw him many curves that often contradict how he imagines his life should proceed. Casual encounters might turn into lifelong friendships, love affairs, important professional contacts, or marriage. A job he failed to get may open him to greater professional possibilities. He'll see, as was the case with Renaissance man James Weldon Johnson and his brother Rosamond, how something he dismissed as not being terribly important might well have great value in the eyes of others and for our culture.

Emery knows nothing at age eight about James Weldon Johnson, and I suspect you, the reader, are not very familiar with his life and work. But we all should be, because when we look at his life, it seems as if we are looking at the biographies of two men, or perhaps three.

He was born in 1871 in Jacksonville, Florida, to a self-educated father who was headwaiter at the St. James Hotel, and a mother who taught at Stanton Public School for Blacks. While attending Atlanta University, Johnson taught the children of former slaves. He and his musician brother Rosamond teamed up with Bob Cole and were remarkably successful songwriters for hit Broadway shows: "The Maiden with the Dreamy Eyes," "My Castle on the Nile," "Under the Bamboo Tree," "The Congo Love Song." He read law books in his leisure time and after some twenty months of doing this became the first black person to pass the Florida Bar exam. During his graduate study at Columbia University, he began writing his classic *The Autobiography of an Ex-Coloured Man*, then completed it while serving as the US Counsel in Venezuela (1906–1909) and Counsel to revolution-racked Nicaragua (1909–1913). Added to that, Johnson ran the editorial page of the *New York Age*, a black, pro-Booker T. Washington newspaper, and served as field secretary for the NAACP, increasing that organization's branches from 68 to 310. Later, in 1920, Johnson became the NAACP's first black general secretary, and lobbied for two years in Congress for the passage of the Dyer Anti-Lynching Bill, which passed in the House, but failed in the Senate.

His was a luminous life, yes—a cornucopia of creativity. After a decade at the NAACP, after writing the important cultural study *Black Manhattan* (1930), editing landmark Harlem Renaissance works like *The Book of American Negro Poetry* (1922), and publishing volumes of verse, Johnson accepted the Adam K. Spence Chair of Creative Literature at Fisk University. His restless intellect and protean talents ended in an automobile accident while he was vacationing in Maine on June 26, 1938.

But it was early in Johnson's life, during his years as principal of the Stanton School in his hometown, that he composed "Lift Ev'ry Voice and Sing" when he was asked to give an address for celebrating Lincoln's birthday.

The song fit young Johnson's nascent aesthetics, which emphasized the fusion of Western forms with black content in order to conjure a new, universal vision of humanity. "I at once recognized the Kiplingesque touch in the two longer lines (of the last stanza); but I knew that in the stanza the American Negro was, historically and spiritually, immanent, and I decided to let it stand as it was written."

With their assignment for the Stanton School completed, the Johnson brothers, never ones to rest on their laurels, quickly moved on to other projects. But it is one of the delicious ironies of an artistic life that the work a creator hopes will be his finest achievement—or his legacy—winds up in history's dustbin while the "lesser" assignment captures a people's American odyssey. In other words, shit happens. Things are impossible to handicap. "The children of Jacksonville were singing the song," he later realized. "Some of them became schoolteachers and taught it to their pupils." Within two decades it was de rigueur, "pasted in the back of hymnals and the songbooks used in Sunday schools, YMCAs," and it was "sung in schools and churches throughout the South and other parts of the country." Johnson, who lived to hear it "fervently sung" even by white students at Bryn Mawr College, confessed, "We wrote better than we knew."

I feel hopeful that Emery will come to appreciate the unpredictable serendipity of life when it goes against our plans and delivers delightful surprises. Disappointment may become gratitude, for as Allen Ginsberg observed, "Clinging to our notion of what we think should be is what causes the 'suffering of suffering.' The suffering itself is not so bad, it's the resentment against suffering that is the real pain."

He'll come to value, too, this thought from Vivekananda (secular people can, if they wish, substitute the word "life" here for God):

When I asked God for Strength
He gave me Difficult Situations to Face
When I asked God for Brain and Brawn
He Gave me Puzzles in Life to Solve
When I asked God for Happiness
He Showed Me Some Unhappy People
When I Asked for Wealth
He Showed Me How to Work Hard
When I Asked God for Peace
He Showed Me How to Help Others
God Gave Me Nothing I Wanted
He Gave Me Everything I Needed.

Opportunities will be plentiful for Emery if he is willing to let go his expectations for what he might believe is perfect for him and open himself to the potentialities of the present moment without expectations. To simply let things *be*. And perhaps, as he does so, to see possibilities that prejudgments closed off for him. His attachment to wanting things to be other than they are will fall away, and he will glimpse the profound meaning in South African President Nelson Mandela's wisdom that "when we can sit in the face of insanity or dislike and be free from the need to make it different, then we are free."

TAT TVAM ASI

When Emery first encounters the Sanskrit saying that serves as the title for this chapter, he may feel confused. It translates as "You are that," and it's certainly not something he will hear every day.

In fact, he might feel such a saying is counterintuitive, given all the divisions and tribalism that he sees today in our society. Almost everyone he encounters, and certainly what he is exposed to in media, will encourage him to see himself as different. However, I want my

grandson to one day realize that *Whatever it is, it's you.*
That whatever he is experiencing, whether it be a person,
place, or thing, he is in one way or another meaningfully
connected to it. He can start probing this connection between himself and others with science. Specifically, he
should begin with a revelation concerning how all of us
can never be more distantly related than fiftieth cousins
in Guy Murchie's *The Seven Mysteries of Life*, a work one
of my students once described as feeling like an entire
college education between the covers of a single book.

"Your own ancestors," Murchie tells us, "whoever
you are, include not only some blacks, some Chinese and
some Arabs, but all the blacks, Chinese, Arabs, Malays,
Latins, Eskimos and every other possible ancestor who
lived on Earth around A.D. 700."

I've pondered for a long time now Murchie's fascinating claim that we need only go back to the year A.D. 700
to discover that no one in the human species can be less
closely related than fiftieth cousins. Our genes, he points
out, circulate throughout the human species in such a
manner that we are joined to everyone once in every fifty
generations. And Murchie cautions us, "If therefore your
appetite disdains any kind of man, shake not your family
tree. For its fruits appear in every color, in every stage of
ripeness or rot, and its branches encompass the earth."

If Emery needs a more immediate demonstration of his

connectedness to others, and if he reads this book by his grandfather, Murchie would hip him to how the book he is holding in his hands was made possible by paper invented in China, by ink created long ago in India, by the invention of type by Germans who used Roman symbols they took from the Greeks who borrowed their letter concepts from Phoenicians who adapted them from Egyptian hieroglyphs.

Science will also introduce Emery to mirror neurons, discovered by Giacomo Rizzolatti and Vittorio Gallese. While research into this area is still very new, and often controversial, I think a thesis worth exploring is advanced by one of its champions, V. S. Ramachandran, a professor of neuroscience at the University of California, San Diego, who posits that mirror neurons are "the starting point for empathy."

In the prefrontal lobes of monkey brains, and presumably in our own brains, the same cells that are activated when performing an action are also activated when watching someone else perform the same action. If Emery sees someone in pain, the anterior cingulate neurons in his brain will cause him to recognize such pain in others and understand it to be like his own experiences of pain. Although not yet empirically proven, I suspect that mirror neurons, which are a subset of motor neurons, not only help us "feel" the pain of others in a kind of virtual reality simulation in ourselves, but also their happiness, love, joy, and other emotions. How many times have you listened to someone, a friend or even a stranger, describe in detail their experience of suffering and found tears welling in your own eyes? Or been moved, as Aristotle says in the *Poetics*, by "pity and fear" in a drama onstage? Or felt such fear when watching a horror movie that you had to avert your eyes? Or felt a powerful emotion sweep over you when listening to the lyrics of a love song? (My own recent favorite is Miten and Premal's "Till I Was Loved by You.")

We all know this experience, because it is what draws us so powerfully to art. "We have never lived enough," philosopher Martha Nussbaum writes in *Love's Knowledge*. "Our experience is, without fiction, too confined and too parochial." All Emery will need to do to understand the truth in this is consider what takes place when he reads.

That experience will be similar to what author Zadie Smith describes in her recent essay "Fascinated to Presume: In Defense of Fiction." Of books, she writes, "I lived in them and felt them living in me. I felt I *was* Jane Eyre and Celie and Mr. Biswas and David Copperfield... I found myself feeling with these imaginary strangers: feeling with them, for them, alongside them and through them, extrapolating from my own emotions, which, though strikingly minor when compared to the high dramas of fiction, still bore some relation to them, as all human feelings do."

Open any novel (or this book in your hands). What is there? Black marks—signs—on white paper. First, they are silent. They are lifeless marks, lacking signification until the consciousness of the reader imbues them with meaning, allowing a fictitious character like Huckleberry Finn, for example, to emerge from the monotonous rows of ebony type. Once this magical act takes place in the mind of the reader, an entire world appears in consciousness: "a vivid and continuous dream," as novelist John Gardner once called this experience, one that so ensorcells us that we forget the room we're sitting in or fail to hear the telephone ringing. In other words, the world experienced within any book is *transcendent*. It exists for consciousness alone. Jean-Paul Sartre says in his book *What is Literature?* that the rare experience found in books is the "conjoint effort of author and reader." While the writer creates their "world" in words, their work requires an attentive reader who will "put himself from the very beginning and almost without a guide at the height of this silence" of signs. Reading, Sartre tells us, is *directed creation*. For each book—each novel or story—requires that a reader exercise their freedom for the "world" and theater of meaning embodied on its pages to *be*. As readers, we invest the cold signs on the pages of Richard Wright's *Native Son* with *our* own emotions, *our* understanding of poverty, oppression, and fear. Then, in what is almost an act of thaumaturgy, the powerful figures and tropes Wright has created reward us richly by returning our subjective feelings to us transformed, refined, and alchemized by language into a new vision with the capacity to change our lives forever.

I'm painting, I suppose, a portrait of our interwoven lives that some cynics might feel is too idealistic. Very well, then. I confess to being an idealist. All my life I've wondered what it would be like to live in a culture where, instead of men and women insulting and tearing down one another, people in their social relations, and even in the smallest ways, held the highest intellectual, moral, creative, and spiritual expectations for one another.

Since our social world is not that way, an idealist must get used to disappointment, especially at this hour in America's culture history when we appear to be obsessed with "otherness." By otherness Emery will come to understand the term is frequently used to refer to *him*, to LGBT people, to women, Jewish people and people of color and virtually everyone who is not a white, Anglo-Saxon Protestant, cisgender, heterosexual male. Straight WASP males, it is often argued, are the recipient of white male privilege, and in this country are the universal human standard against which all others are consciously or unconsciously measured. The glaring absurdity of this notion is evident when we consider that people of color make up between 70 and 83 percent of the world's population while whites account for between 17 and 30 percent. I cannot deny, and have no interest in denying, that until quite recently this very racist propaganda, which was subtly and sometimes blatantly promoted in American and European societies since at least the eighteenth century, was a lie that could be found everywhere. It is behind the spurious justifications for slavery, racial segregation, colonialism, and the terrible treatment of everyone who in any way differed from cisgender, white men.

At this writing, the agonies associated with otherness have polarized Americans in a way perhaps impossible to repair. The phrase *e pluribus unum*, or "out of many, one," can today seem like a cruel joke. The pain caused by our obsession with racial, gender, and sexual otherness, in the past and present, has fueled various forms of tribalism, ideologies based on difference, and led to the sickening mass killings of black Americans in churches and Jews in synagogues.

My hope is that Emery will remember a story I read in my teens, which I will share with him, about D. T. Suzuki, the major interpreter of Zen Buddhism in the middle of the twentieth century.

As the story goes, Dr. Suzuki was giving a lecture, and during the Q&A, a member of the audience asked him, "Dr. Suzuki, what about the Other?" Suzuki became quiet. He thought long and hard about the question, there at the podium. After a time, he put his head down on his folded arms, and only after a few minutes did he lift it. He looked at the person who'd asked him the question, and replied, "*What* Other?"

In Buddhism, there is no dualism between self and Other. Indeed, there is no self—that is an illusion, a social construct—and there is no "Other" either. Science also denies the existence of such an entity as a substance—rather, we are simply consciousness, thoughts without a "thinker." Suzuki paused and thought for so long because in Buddha Dharma the question simply made no sense.

As he grows in maturity, I think my grandson in his inevitable acceptance of the reality that nothing is personal, permanent, or perfect, will also ideally grow in humility and compassion. He will understand our limitations as C. S. Lewis described them: "Five senses; an incurably abstract intellect; a haphazardly selective memory; a set of preconceptions and assumptions so numerous that I can never examine more than a minority of them—never become conscious of them all. How much of total reality can such an apparatus let through?"

But he will recognize, even with these limitations, his connectedness to everything supposedly "other," and that nothing can be a stranger or alien to him.

"A human being is part of the whole, called by us 'universe,' a part limited in time and space," Albert Einstein once wrote. "He experiences himself, his thoughts and feelings, as something separate from the rest—a kind of optical delusion of his consciousness. This delusion is a kind of prison for us, restricting us to our personal desires and to affection for a few persons nearest to us. Our task must be to free ourselves from this prison by widening our circle of compassion to embrace all living creatures and the whole of nature in its beauty."

May our grandchildren break free of the "prison" Einstein spoke of and rise to the occasion of the task he placed before us.

THE THREE DIMENSIONS OF A COMPLETE LIFE

S omeday I expect my grandson Emery to ask me about America's most celebrated civil rights leader, Martin Luther King Jr. About who he was and what he did. And what he should mean for us today, because we have canonized King. He is both the creator and product of a moment in history, the American symbol for the struggle against segregation. The ideal of integration wears his face. He is someone who we think we know—this nation's preacher and our most prominent moral philosopher, but for the most part he is only presented to us as a civil rights leader for black Americans. Across this country, his photograph is on display in elementary and secondary schools. It's difficult to visit a major American city and not find a street or public building named after him. Most of our states honor the national holiday established in his name. And a huge statue in his honor rests on the National Mall.

But despite the overwhelming presence of this man in our lives, significant dimensions of him are strangely absent. Even though I grew up in the 1960s, and even though I remember the day he was killed in 1968, it wasn't until the 1980s that I realized how little I knew about this man, although I often invoked his name. But what was his intellectual and spiritual development? I knew the end result of his political thinking but nothing about the steps that led him there. So for me in 1990, I felt the private man we call Martin Luther King Jr. had over time become a cultural object difficult to grasp in his individuality, in his humanness, and in the minutiae of his daily life, and I found this ironic because these are the very foundations from which a public life arises. The only solution to this for me was to spend seven years immersing myself in research about him, writing my fourth novel, *Dreamer*, which examines his only northern campaign in Chicago, among other things, then composing a short story and essays about him, and delivering many speeches across America on his eponymous holiday. Before I was done, I'd devoted a fifth of my life to King's memory and achievements.

I will tell Emery that King was a preacher, but that I did not know before I started writing *Dreamer* what his favorite passages were in the Bible, for example, the passage in the Gospel of Mark that described an exchange between Jesus and the apostles John and James. I didn't know in what ways he agreed or disagreed with the religious thinkers he studied, people like Walter Rauschenbusch, Reinhold Niebuhr, and Paul Tillich. That I didn't know what novels and motion pictures he enjoyed. And that I wasn't aware of how deeply racial politics was in his blood, that he imbibed resistance to injustice nearly every night at the dinner table, where King Sr. discussed politics with his family.

Until the 1990s, I did not know his father counseled young Martin against feelings of class superiority, or that he did manual labor during the Depression, and from his childhood was unable to make his peace with capitalism. And this was only the beginning of my ignorance about King.

We quote King often to make a point about oppression, never the King who counseled black students in Chicago in 1964 that "when you're behind in a footrace, the only way to get ahead is to run faster than the man in front of you. So when your white roommate says he is tired and goes to sleep, you stay up and burn the midnight oil."

I realized I didn't know the very things every novelist must know when he creates a character: namely, King's personal habits, his likes and dislikes, his idiosyncrasies, his deepest feelings of shame and triumph, his obsessions and compulsions.

For example, what did he like to drink? (Apparently, on one occasion he liked orange juice and vodka.) How did he shave when he got up in the morning? (From what I read, Martin's skin was too sensitive for a razor, as my own skin is, and he shaved with a smelling powder called "Magic," which many black men today still use.) But to write *Dreamer* I needed to know much more than that. I needed to know the compositional logic of the way he used language as well as the sources behind his rhetoric, influences such as the sermons of J. Wallace Hamilton, Harry Emerson Fosdick, Harold Bosley, and those of King's own father. In order to focus the novel on the years between 1966 and 1968 when King brought the Freedom Movement to the Chicago area, I had to bring myself to identify completely with the man who came away from that campaign less than satisfied with its success, who had a $30,000 bounty on his head, who lamented the death of Malcolm X, despaired over the growing racial polarization in America, who saw young black power activists like Stokely Carmichael making deeper inroads into urban black America than he could, though King kept expanding his agenda by taking on the war in Vietnam and Lyndon Johnson, and organizing a massive poor people's march on the nation's capital.

I needed to know the King who walked across this minefield for thirteen years and toward the end of his life said to his longtime friend and ally Bayard Rustin, "Bayard, I sometimes wonder where I can go from here… What can I do now." And last of all, I needed to know—from the inside—the King who believed in the interrelatedness of all things and the "inescapable network of mutuality" that binds all people in "a single garment of destiny."

I came to see that if I really intended to probe deeper into King's vision and values, I would also be compelled to probe into a bygone era of black American cultural history—one that my father and mother and their friends from South Carolina and Georgia knew well, but which was fast slipping away by the early 1960s when I came of age. And there's no way Emery or someone of his generation can know firsthand that the '60s were an extremely violent decade of political assassinations (JFK, RFK, MLK, Malcolm X, Fred Hampton, and so many others), or that the federal government was considering what to do in the event of civil war—specifically, race war. It was also a time of theater and the rise of television culture (which broadcast King's campaigns to the entire world).

I will have to explain to my grandson that I worried if the entire man, King, could be recovered in a work of fiction. I'll tell him that I sometimes wondered if this was even possible when we seem to have such difficulty understanding even the lives of those people closest to us. Given that difficulty, I decided that the most important thing was to capture, if possible, the *eidos* (or essence) of his life. The urgency I felt when writing *Dreamer* was real because what was at stake in the Martin Luther King Jr. story—and in the story of the Civil Rights Movement—were not only questions about American race relations but also deeper questions, older questions about the nature of moral action, about what it means to be human, about cultural identity, and the challenge of ending social evils without creating new social evils.

I'll tell Emery that when I looked at King, when I remembered the portrait of him that my parents had in our house in Evanston, and when I considered that his sacrifices and those of thousands of others in the Civil Rights Movement made it possible for me to attend college, I realized that I was a child of integration. It was an ideal I took for granted all throughout high school and college. Yet it was replaced briefly in me by a flirtation with black cultural nationalism during my college years before I fully had the chance to subject the black American goal of integration to philosophical examination. What that means is I was not fully living an examined life, nor would I be able to do that until I returned to those last years of Martin's life and took up the problems and passions that concerned him on the day he was cut down at the Lorraine in Memphis. Put another way, what was at stake was the very practical manner of how I would live the remainder of my life in the 1990s until today, and what I honestly felt I could teach my future grandson about the social world, and about what is good and what is evil.

So, yes, one day Emery will have to "make a witness" to King, though not as thoroughly as I attempted to do. I'm going to suggest that he start with one of King's favorite sermons, "The Three Dimensions of a Complete Life." This is the sermon that earned King his first job as pastor at Dexter Avenue Baptist Church in Montgomery, Alabama, which he also delivered at St. Paul's Cathedral in London on his way to receive the Nobel Peace Prize.

In this speech, King summarizes the Jewish rabbi Joshua Liebman, who wrote a book some years ago titled *Peace of Mind*. The rabbi has a chapter in that book, "Love Thyself Properly." What he says in substance is that before you can love others adequately, you've got to love your own self properly. This simple advice is often hard to remember. We know it's right to care for others. But sometimes in doing so we can neglect self-care and place the happiness of others ahead of our own happiness. Such self-deprecation is unhealthy. We must love ourselves as we do others, and for King, this "means that you've got to accept yourself. So many people are busy trying to be somebody else."

We know, of course, that we can't be somebody else, because everybody else is taken. But being oneself demands that we "discover what we are called to do. And once we discover it we should set out to do it with all of the strength and all of the power we have in our systems...we should set out to do that work so well that the living, the dead, or the unborn couldn't do it any better." This is what so saddened me about the gentleman I met on Bainbridge Island, who had spent his life searching for his passion, for what he was "called to do." Looking back on that encounter, I wish I'd had a copy of this sermon by King to give to him, and to add that we know what we are "called to do" by the weight we feel inside us, in our hearts and minds, for that work, even if no one around us can understand our passion. It brings us joy, a sense of fulfillment, but there is also a sense in which we surrender to it, accepting it as we accept the inevitability of ourselves.

I know I will need to caution my grandson against the desire to be "great." Naturally, we all wish to turn in a great performance in whatever we do. But as a friend once said to me, "the great is the enemy of the good." Too much concern about doing something great can blind us to the value of simply delivering a performance that is good. One shouldn't overreach. Another friend of mine once used a metaphor about some creative people having too many planes on the runway and not managing to get any of them into the air. Sometimes, I'll explain to my grandson, less *is* more.

But King would not be King if his sermon stopped with self-care. He heaps considerable scorn on those who "try to live as if nobody else lives in the world but themselves. And they use everybody as mere tools to get where they're going. They don't love anybody but themselves. And the only kind of love that they really have for other people is utilitarian love. You know, they just love people that they can use."

It is in this section that King calls forth a beautiful passage that in his own words fuses the Buddhist sense of *pratitya samutpada* or "interconnectedness" with Murchie's science-based insight into how our lives are really characterized by a We-relation. King preached:

We're tied together in life and in the world. And you may think you got all you got by yourself. But you know, before you got here to church this morning, you were dependent on more than half of the world. You get up in the morning and go to the bathroom, and you reach over for a bar of soap, and that's handed to you by a Frenchman. You reach over for a sponge, and that's given to you by a Turk.

King gives more examples and concludes:

Before you get through eating breakfast in the morning, you're dependent on more than half the world... So let us be concerned about others because we are dependent on others.

The third dimension of life, said King, is the quest for the divine, because "we were made for God, and we will be restless until we find rest in him."

Like King, Emery—and all of us—should never ignore the spiritual register in our lives.

SUFFERING
IS VOLUNTARY
OR OPTIONAL

My friend Seattle writer Brian McDonald tells a story that I know I will share with my grandson. It is a story about the tragic murder of his brother Brent in the early-morning hours on December 14, 2015. And it is about how Brian processed this personal loss.

As background for this story, you should know that McDonald is a superb teacher of storytelling techniques, particularly in the field of motion pictures. He is the author of two excellent books, *Invisible Ink: A Practical Guide to Building Stories That Resonate* and *The Golden Theme: How to Make Your Writing Appeal to the Highest Common Denominator.* McDonald has taught his story-structure seminars at Pixar, Disney Feature Animation, and Lucasfilm's ILM. He is an award-winning director/writer who has written comic books and graphic novels, for A&E's *Hoarders*, and has directed spots for Visa. His highly entertaining film *White Face*, which imagines what it would be like if circus clowns were a separate race, has run on HBO and Cinemax, and is used nationwide by corporations as a tool for diversity training. Presently, he holds the title of chief storyteller at Belief Agency in Seattle.

Some years ago I received an email from Brian that rocked me back in my chair and left me reeling. He said his brother Brent, an art teacher, had just been killed on a sidewalk in the Belltown neighborhood of Seattle. The shooting was random. The killer, a man named Richard Roundtree, didn't know Brent and fired as they approached each other on the street. McDonald attended the trial of his brother's killer. In a moving talk he gave, which is available online, he explains that when it was Roundtree's time to take the stand, a woman he didn't know said, "Great, now we get to hear again how hard it is to be a crack dealer." Apparently, she recoiled at the prospect of listening to Brent's killer, but McDonald says he wanted to hear this man's story. Despite the pain he must have felt, he truly wanted to understand Roundtree, what his life and motives might have been, because Brian McDonald is, first and foremost, a storyteller, which means he is a student of characters, i.e., people and what makes them tick.

As McDonald listened to Roundtree, he learned that his brother's killer was born in South Central LA into a gang family that helped found the Crips. When Roundtree was only six years old, his father went to prison for shooting a police officer during a robbery. Roundtree himself had been in prison for selling drugs to support his family. Naturally, he didn't like prison, and so he apparently tried to learn a trade. But when he was released, he couldn't find a job because he was a convicted felon. That led him back to selling drugs, and one night he was badly stabbed. According to Roundtree, he felt threatened when Brent McDonald came walking toward him and wouldn't get out of the way.

"How," McDonald asks in the video of his talk, "could I empathize with this guy?"

How, indeed.

Looking at his own life, McDonald says, he found parallels between the rejection he'd received as a young black man and the circumstances of Roundtree's troubled life. His teachers, he said, were "prepared to throw me away." He came to feel that "it wasn't a big leap for me to have empathy... I was angry at the system that wouldn't give Richard Roundtree a job. I was angry at the system that wouldn't educate him. I was angry at the system that created the poverty that created him."

During the trial of Richard Roundtree, the King County Superior Court judge Hollis Hill, who would decide on the punishment for Roundtree, asked for letters from those affected by this murder. Judge Hill was so moved by McDonald's letter that she referenced it when she delivered the sentence.

"I have been thinking about justice and I realize I have no idea what the word means," wrote McDonald. "We so often use it to mean vengeance but I haven't the stomach for vengeance. I discovered after my brother was killed that hatred does not come easily to me.

"I should explain that when I heard the defense for Mr. Roundtree I did not hear something that was completely bogus or without merit. This is not to say I think he had cause to murder my brother, but it is to say that being a black man in America I know all of the pressures that can push one into making horrible life choices.

"Both Brent and I were bussed to West Seattle high school in the early 80s. The school was rampant with racism—and I'm not talking about students—I'm talking about faculty. My first day at that school I had a teacher say to me that although she had not seen me do anything wrong she was sure that I had.

"This kind of thing was par for the course at that school.

"I have no idea of the forces that shaped Mr. Roundtree. He is slightly older than I am which means he undoubtedly suffered many of the same indignities that Brent and I did. Those who don't have to suffer the constant insults and slights and just plain injustices that occur because one walks around in black skin have a hard time comprehending what it does to one's psyche. Sometimes the path of least resistance is to live down to the expectations others have of you. The struggle to prove your worth or humanity can sometimes be a heavy load and sometimes people break under the strain.

"For all I know Mr. Roundtree grew up in a house full of lead paint as so many poor children of color have. Or maybe he grew up in a house without love in addition to the prejudice he experienced in the world outside of his home. I don't know.

"I wish we, as a society, would take care of these injustices when society is perpetuating them against little kids. Because we don't bother to do that, my brother is dead and Mr. Roundtree will more than likely spend the rest of his life in jail. For me this is two wasted lives.

"I guess I'm saying I wish we had a different system. But this is the system we have.

"There is no sentence that will bring back my mother's child. There is no sentence that will bring back the nephew of my aunts and uncles. There is no sentence that will bring back the beloved art teacher. There is no sentence that will bring back the stepson. There is no sentence that will bring back my brother.

"I hope you understand that there is no doubt in my mind that Mr. Roundtree killed my brother in cold blood. He seemed to have no remorse at all. All I can think is that someone without empathy must've been hurt very deeply and probably very young.

"I ask you for a sentence that keeps this man from hurting anyone else. No part of me feels any pleasure in this request. I wish we could've helped a boy rather than punish the man, but this is what we call justice, I guess."

In the video of his talk, McDonald concludes that "Richard Roundtree was just the person who pulled the trigger. It was the system that killed my brother. I know that little black boys are thrown away every day."

According to McDonald, some people have called the way he came to terms with his brother's murder "saintly." He denies it, and perhaps because he understands that pain is an inevitable part of life, but suffering is voluntary or optional. In other words, we cannot avoid painful experiences during our journey through life. But we are always free to decide how we shall react to them—if, as in McDonald's case, we will choose vengeance or the more difficult but ultimately healing approach of empathy.

McDonald identifies a "system" of racism and throwing little black boys away as the real killer of his brother. No one can—or should—deny the truth he speaks. There are too many fatherless black boys growing up in homes without love, and in poverty. There are too many attending (or not attending) schools where they are just warehoused until graduation, and where they don't receive the skills they need to be competitive and successful in society. This is no longer a problem for black America. Long ago it became a tragic *condition* for too many of our children.

McDonald's truths can be found in the brilliant works of Ralph Ellison, Jared Walker, Stanley Crouch, Albert Murray, and Clifford Thompson (a clear-thinking and courageous essayist who had Murray as his mentor). In his latest book, *What It Is: Race, Family, and One Thinking Black Man's Blues*, Thompson relates an incident where he says this to his sister about white people: "They hate us." And she wisely replies, "Just remember they're not all the same." Nor have all white Americans been the same, or racists, since the founding of this republic. How many have exhibited their love for a black person in marriage? Through adoption? Or raising as white grandparents the future president Barack Obama? By mentoring and championing black individuals in whom they saw talent, high intelligence, and a strong work ethic? To suggest such white individuals have not existed since the colonial era is to suppress a profile that is simply too great to ignore.

But I would do wrong, and I would lie, if I told Emery that the pain we experience in life will completely heal. Time and distance from a painful event may gradually weaken it as the years, then decades go by. But it is likely that the pain will remain in our memories, and we may wear scar tissue for the rest of our lives. This is as it must be. This is what it means to be human, and to experience a more perfectly realized broken heart when we see ourselves potentially in every victim and victimizer, in every slayer and the slain. As a superb analyst of stories and the characters that animate them, Brian McDonald goes where many others fail to go because—as a writer, as a person— he has trained himself to try his best to inhabit imaginatively and with empathy every life he encounters, on and off the page, despite how painful that might be. At this writing, he is hard at work on a graphic memoir about his brother's murder. I dare say McDonald gives us an example worthy of my grandson's—and all of our—admiration.

6

EXPERIENCE SOMETHING BEAUTIFUL EVERY DAY

I will insist that my grandson include the experience of beauty in his life every day, whether that be through music, nature, a painting, literature, or anywhere he can find it in a world that offers too much in the way of ugliness, falsity, confusion, delusion, and evil. So much that is beautiful may be right outside his window.

I would love to see eleven years from now my grandson's high school graduation ceremony. When he turns eighteen, I will be an old geezer at age eighty-two years old, about the age my father was when he passed away. I plan on being at that ceremony. But what if I'm not? What if I've left life's stage before Emery reaches his teens? Well, his grandfather *is* by trade a storyteller. So I plan on leaving him a story about one bad day in a Seattle teenager's life, a day that ends with his experience of beauty putting him on the path to liberation.

Kubota Garden: A Zen Sketch

It was the end of the day at a private high school in Burien. Seventeen-year-old Joshua Davis was in the locker room, changing out of his sweats—Coach Williams had his class run around the track five times before soccer practice—and Joshua was putting on his street clothes when he heard the voice of Eli Jenson behind him.

"Hey, Joshua," he said. "Why don't you cut off those dreadlocks? You'd see the ball better if they weren't swinging in your face."

Joshua felt his stomach clench and his lungs tighten, but he ignored Eli. He didn't want trouble. He just wanted to go home after a long day at school. But Eli was always messing with him.

"Did you hear me?" said Eli, stepping closer. "Those stringy dreads make you look like that monster Miss Cummings talked about in our mythology class. What's her name? Medusa. And you know you're ugly enough already!"

Then Eli grabbed a fistful of Joshua's dreads and pulled on them from behind, painfully snapping back his head. Right then, Joshua was on him. Pounding on Eli with a flurry of punches in an elixir of rage and hatred that frightened even Joshua himself. Blossoms of blood spread across his knuckles. And, as luck would have it, at just that moment, Coach Williams came into the locker room. He pulled the boys apart, yelling that he wouldn't tolerate fighting in his gym. Then he hauled Joshua and Eli to the principal's office. And *he*, furious and red-faced and puffing up like a blowfish, suspended both boys for a day.

Now, the last thing Joshua wanted to do was go home to face his parents. They weren't wealthy, but they scrimped and saved to keep him in a private school and away from kids they considered a bad influence. He knew they didn't want him to be just another sad statistic. Or funneled into the school-to-prison pipeline. So far their gamble was paying off. His teachers liked him, and he was doing well academically, even though he often felt lonely, because he was one of only five black students in what felt sometimes like a vanilla sea of well-off, privileged kids so different from him. A couple were his friends in the chess club, and on the school newspaper, where he sometimes published his poems.

But after school, as he walked slowly along Renton Avenue South, his backpack stuffed with fat textbooks that felt heavier with every step, he wondered for the hundredth time where he belonged. Or if he belonged anywhere. At school, he felt self-conscious and lost. His counselor, Mrs. Daniels, said to him, "Joshua, I've noticed that you're always pretty relaxed, but you never *completely* relax." He got silent when she said that because it was true—he never let down his guard. At school, he never relaxed completely, and he knew he didn't have the luxury of clowning around like the other kids, because his parents had already given him the Talk every young black male one day has to receive.

His father told him that if the other kids went into the bathroom to drink or do a little dope, that was fine for them, but if *he* did those things and got caught messing up in a country like America, with its double standards for whites and people of color, his punishment would be far more severe than it would be for them. And if he ever went to jail, they didn't have the money or connections to bribe a judge to bail him out. So, no. He knew he didn't have the luxury of making mistakes. Or completely relaxing when he stepped outside his parents' home. And back in the hood, he had to be careful not to sound too

bookish or nerdy around other kids. Before saying anything, he had to quickly think before he spoke, selecting
his words as carefully as a poet might, so people wouldn't
think he was putting on airs by using words, phrases, or
ideas they didn't know. In both worlds Joshua felt like an
outsider. Or someone on a tightrope. It was as if he wore
a mask at school and another one in the hood. Walking home, he felt a twinge of anger at everything that
moved. He trembled at the thought of what he might
have done to Eli. And almost every day he wondered:
Who am I? What am I? How can I survive, feeling split
in half this way?

No, he didn't want to tell his parents he'd been kicked
out of school. His family had lived in Rainier Beach for
less than a year so parts of the neighborhood were still
new for him, like the road he only now noticed snak-
ing away from the street. At its entrance sat a big rock
outlined in gold by the late afternoon light. It was en-
graved with Japanese characters, and below them the
words *Kubota Garden*. Curious, he let his feet carry him
eastward toward the entrance. With each step away from
Renton Avenue, as he moved closer to the Garden's wel-
coming gate, the world seemed to grow quieter the way
he felt whenever he entered a sacred place like his parents' church, with the noise of traffic and city sounds
being replaced by a hymnal stillness. In a similar way,

with each step he took toward the Garden, the constant background static and congestion of his thoughts, the obsessive memories and fears, hopes and desires—*that* inner racket began to fade away like puffs of smoke scattered by the gentlest of breezes.

As he picked up a few pamphlets inside the entry gate on the history of the Garden, he noticed how the brilliant Japanese maples and madronas and still-new blond pines made the air he inhaled so oxygen-rich the space behind his eyes and between his ears began to feel clearer, less tight, and he remembered something said by his science teacher, Mr. Smith: One acre of forest absorbs six tons of carbon dioxide and emits four tons of oxygen, which was enough to meet the needs of eighteen people.

Inside the entrance now, he saw a sign inviting him to strike a bronze bell with a wooden mallet, and he did so, the sound vibrating in the cavity of his chest. Then he saw paths winding away to his left and right. Which one to choose? Joshua wasn't sure so he just went to the left. But after only a few seconds of walking on a path of leaf-filtered light designed to simultaneously conceal and reveal Nature's generosity, he emerged from a section of forest into an opening that made him stop and stare. Just stare, for he had fallen into what felt like a sensuous poem, a profound mystery, and at its center was a large spirit stone. Its density, the heaviness of it, seemed to bend space and time around itself. He stood silently before it, forced by its presence to listen since he was unexpectedly part of a vignette of stone, emptiness, water, plants, and…Joshua. The rough stone, with its tonsured top and wide center, seemed to have its own personality, and was the focal point and bone structure of the scene in which he found himself. It was probably hundreds of years old, older than America, very old, and held secrets Joshua felt he could not begin to imagine.

There were lessons to be learned here, he realized, and then he wondered how had this forest, so different from the rest of Seattle and hiding in plain sight, come to be? Joshua let his heavy backpack slide off his shoulder to the ground and sat down by the stone. Others quietly visiting the Garden gave him a friendly nod as they walked the paths. They were Vietnamese, Somalis, Filipinos, black Americans, whites, and Latinos, slow walking and letting the twenty acres of forest bathe them with its spirit. He opened the pamphlet he picked up at the entrance and began to read a remarkable story he shamefully knew nothing about.

Long ago, or so he read, this place where he sat had been a stinking swamp, a waste area of tangled brush in Upper Rainier Beach. Mapes Creek coursed through it. No one believed the place had any value. Not until Fujitaro Kubota immigrated from the small Japanese island of

Shikoku to Hawaii in 1907, from there to San Francisco, then up the coast to the sawmills in Selleck, and finally to Seattle, where he for a time managed hotels and apartment buildings in a segregated area that would one day become the International District. With his free time, he helped friends in the gardening business, discovered this sort of work brought him both pleasure and peace, and in 1923 founded the Kubota Gardening Company. When he looked at the five acres of swamp with the eyes of an artist, for Fujitaro was an amateur Kabuki actor, often taking the role of female characters, and was also a singer in the Japanese Gidayu tradition—when *those* eyes took in what so many others had ignored, he envisioned it as perfect showcase for his nursery, a place to demonstrate to his clients the kinds of gardens he could create for them in the spirit of Buddhism and Konkokyo, the branch of Shintoism he belonged to, one devoted to achieving spiritual awakening through the experience of nature. Draining the swamp required the hot work of digging a trench ten feet deep, but once that was done, he envisioned where he stood as a serene place for meditation where Japanese families and others prohibited from enjoying full citizenship in Seattle might find a retreat from worldly conflicts. A place that reconciled opposites, transcended the dualities that divided humankind, and, most important of all, provided a Way, or Dao, for visitors to merge their hearts and minds with heaven and earth.

But then came World War II.

In 1942, Fujitaro and all members of his family were ordered to relocate to an internment camp in Idaho. It was called the Minidoka War Relocation Center. Predictably, the camp was bleak, on barren desert land, and surrounded by an electrified barbed wire fence. Japanese citizens had to take loyalty oaths. Some became No-No Boys by refusing to answer the last two questions about loyalty and serving in the military, but Fujitaro's two sons, Tak and Thomas, decided to become translators and instructors in the army. And he, based on his work in Seattle, became the camp's chief gardener in charge of beautification projects. Even though he suffered greatly during his three years of internment, Fujitaro created an entrance garden that featured an honor roll board for the 418 Japanese Americans who left their families in Minidoka to serve in the US military, as his sons had done. Today that internment camp garden is the site for a yearly pilgrimage for those who want to learn about this dark chapter in America's history.

Joshua read next about Kubota's return to Seattle in 1945. When he saw what remained of his original Garden, his eyes burned with tears. Weeds and kudzu choked the roads. The once-beautiful ponds were filled with trash, effluvium, and the stench of swamp water. And yet those three years of neglect suggested to Kubota's artistic eyes the possibility for something unique, spontaneous, and with a touch of serendipity that traditional Japanese gardens did not possess. Never trained in Japan in the time-honored ways of gardening there (the old masters refused to share their secrets with him), and never one to work with a pre-established blueprint, but instead someone conditioned by Shintoism and Zen to listen to nature, Fujitaro saw how the wild growth, uncultivated and bursting with variety, might complement the delicate order conceived by his own sensibility. Nature and mind *could* balance each other like yin and yang.

Using a scythe, he cut away weeds high as his waist, but of course they weren't all *that* high because Fujitaro was only four feet eleven inches tall. Yet his spirit was expansive, and by virtue of that the Garden expanded to the twenty-plus acres in which Joshua found himself.

He slipped the pamphlet into his backpack. A thought burst to the surface of his mind, like koi fish breaking the surface of the Garden's ponds: There could be no beauty without ugliness. No success without failure. No pleasure without pain, or life without death. These twins were forever linked like sunlight and shade. Something in Joshua began to relax. His thoughts drifted to the internment camp in Idaho. Slavery a century before was an unspeakable evil for his ancestors. And racial segregation was a seventy-year violation of everything this country said it stood for. But Kubota—as much an outsider as Joshua felt himself to be—had not given up hope, despite the fact that in 1927 he was not a naturalized American citizen, and therefore could not buy those first five acres of land. So he had a friend secure the land for him. Joshua saw that once these obstacles were overcome, Kubota's deeds spread seeds of beauty that flowered as far away as the Seattle Center, the Japanese Garden at Blodel Reserve, the Rainier Club, and at Seattle University. He, once excluded, let anyone come to his ever-changing Garden. That Joshua found fascinating, because it seemed to suggest that, like the neglected Garden during the war years, America's swamp of social injustice was strangely enough the precondition for creating people of color determined to act in a generous spirit exactly opposite that of those who oppressed them.

As he walked slowly, letting the forest paths of gravel and stone guide his feet, that old, nagging feeling of himself separated from others began to fall away. He felt just maybe he *could* return hate with love, and meanness with kindness as Kubota did. But he felt something more, too. The bright, translucent air was so oxygenated, the forceps of his attention focused now on his breaths, how each was different. Some shallow, some deep, some warm, some cool, with every in-breath or exhale fresh and new. For Kubota's Garden awakened him to the fact that he was essentially and inescapably a body among so many other bodies—cherry blossoms that still held the knoll of the bell he'd struck, lanterns, bridges, hedges, shrubs, and the miraculous gift of far-reaching trees that were colossi towering above him. This felt like a spiritualized sensuality, because walking these acres was an aerobic experience that had him suddenly descending slopes on steps made of rocks, and climbing hills that did not so much rise as they sheered skyward in rippling planes, and so he had to place his feet down ever so carefully if he didn't want to slip or fall, and that let him feel with every footfall the firmness of the earth meeting and pressing back to balance each of his movements. It was strange to say, maybe even to *think*, but it felt to Joshua that everything that was and ever had been was here. Always changing form, but here, nevertheless.

He moved on through Kubota's work of art, made of what he was made, finding and losing himself at the same time in the rhythms of emptiness and forms. Through the Fera Fera Forest, the Tom Kubota Stroll Garden, the Japanese Garden with its Kasuga stone lantern, and the Moon Bridge that represented in a wizardly light how hard it is to lead a good life with the words "Hard to walk up and hard to walk down." Joshua realized he was the tiniest of figures blending into this picture, beneath a canopy of empty sky that seemed endless, growing darker now as night came on. Feeling a little winded, breathing high in his lungs, he sat down on a bench near a fossil stone forty million years old, just below a waterfall and near a pond. Whatever feelings of anger and fear that had overwhelmed him thinned and disappeared, as if they never were. Eli Jenson's taunts were as far removed from his mind as the man in the moon.

Quietly, he sat, breathing slowly, letting his guard down, dropping deeper into his embodiment, feeling as if his earlier fight happened in another life, or to someone else—someone he no longer was, or certainly was not at this moment. Every moment was different in the Garden. And so was he. Right here, right now he was the spill of early-evening light on delicate leaves lighter than a whisper, the sinewy bark of trees that reminded him of the wrinkled skin of elephants, the breeze feathering pond water into ripples, the muffled brooling of the waterfall Kubota had created, the water flowing freely, capable of assuming the shape of anything. Joshua felt he could do that now, for in just this past hour the Garden had nourished his spirit, showing him the littleness of what people called "race" in the vastness of Being. That made him smile because he, so aware of his body now, knew that one day he would come back to this place, this Earth, like a raindrop falling back into the sea, and nourish it as it did him now.

And underneath it all, *underneath it all*, he could hear the Garden whisper gently that he would never die.

He pulled his cell phone from his backpack and checked the time. Eight p.m. It was finally time to leave this place where he felt he fit so well and go home. To face his parents. He wasn't going to fool himself about how they would react to his suspension. He knew they would go ballistic as the numinous Garden lingered in his mind. And that was all right. That thought no longer frightened him.

Nothing did.

7

OPEN MOUTH, ALREADY A MISTAKE

An enormous number of books on Buddhism have been published, but one of my favorite titles is the one that begins this chapter, from a book by Zen master Wu Kwang. It resonates perfectly with Muslim wisdom I've encountered that tells us that before we speak, we should pass whatever we intend to say through three gatekeepers. The three gatekeepers are questions. Is what we are about to say *true*? Is it *necessary* (to say currently)? And will it *do no harm*? I intend to tell my grandson that if our speech can pass these three gates, it is worthy of sharing with others.

On October 1, 2019, the followers of the late spiritual teacher Eknath Easwaran, who often speak in his name and using his words, posted a "thought for the day" regarding this Arab proverb:

It is so easy to say something at the expense of another for the purpose of enhancing our own image. But such remarks—irresistible as they may be—serve only to fatten our egos and agitate others. We should be so fearful of hurting people that even if a clever remark is rushing off our tongue, we can barricade the gate. We should be able to swallow our cleverness rather than hurt someone. Better to say something banal but harmless than to be clever at someone else's expense.

In addition to the Three Gates, I believe my grandson should learn something about the classic logical fallacies that we are exposed to every day. I would not have encountered them if I had not been a journalism major during my undergraduate years. All journalism majors at my university in 1966 were required to take a course titled "Introduction to Logic," and it was during that course in logic that my eighteen-year-old eyes were opened. My teachers wisely understood that if one was going to becoming a journalist, a newspaper reporter, then he or she *better* know something about the logical fallacies constantly appearing in "arguments" by politicians. And also in advertising. Furthermore, a grounding in the logical fallacies was superb preparation for anyone who wished to engage in debate, and for future lawyers. That first year I was in college and took Introduction to Logic, I realized I'd been handed an antidote for all the illogical statements I remembered people making all around me as I was growing up. Armed with this information, I felt, to use some black American slang here, that I'd never be a "chump." And no one would be able to "bump my head."

My friend philosopher Michael Boylan is even more emphatic about this in his book *The Process of Argument: An Introduction*, when he writes, "Like logical arguments, logical fallacy seeks to persuade. The problem is that its means are not legitimate. It uses trick and sleights of hand to distract and confuse while the audience is being manipulated. To be manipulated is to become that person's slave."

I'm sure none of us wish to be a slave. But I suspect most Americans have never taken a course in logic. During my decades of teaching creative writing, I often gave my students a handout I put together with the title "45 Logical Fallacies." I once asked my students if anyone had taken a logic course. At best, only two people out of twenty might raise their hands. One day I will share a shortened version of this handout with Emery, highlighting fourteen of the ways our thinking slips into non-sense:

1. Emery should be skeptical whenever he hears someone who **generalizes** or speaks in **absolute** terms, or whenever he hears someone lump all members of any group together, suggesting that they think or believe the same things. For example, "All women are…" or "All men are…" or "All Muslims are…" When he hears someone generalize or make a sweeping statement, he should ask if the generalization is based on a **sample** that is large enough and not atypical or peculiar.

2. He should be aware of **special pleading** when he hears it, that is, when someone presents an argument or case without also showing its drawbacks, faults, or problems.

3. My grandson should also be conscious of when in an **argument by coercion** he is not being given objective facts based on evidence but instead is being subtly (or not so subtly) bullied, threatened, or the speaker hopes to instill fear in him, as in "If you don't go on a diet and

lose all that excess weight, you're going to get sick." A variation on this is an **appeal to guilt**. "You're doing fine—you've been lucky—so you must help those less fortunate." Other spins on this fallacy are an **appeal to pity** ("Your Honor, you should give my client a lighter sentence because he had a miserable childhood"), and to **popular sentiment**, as when a speaker says, "Everybody does it so you should do it, too." An interesting spin on that one is called **Tu quoque**, where someone says, "You can't argue against me, because *you* do the same thing yourself."

4. Emery should recognize immediately when, in his discussions with others, they subject his position to **extension**, that is, when in the language they use they exaggerate what he is saying in order to make it more vulnerable. A variation on this is when they misrepresent what he is saying, creating a **straw man** easy for the other person to defeat in argumentation. Yet another fallacy he should watch out for is when someone he is speaking to engages in **Misuse of Humor** to get an audience to laugh and forget his argument and its seriousness.

5. A fallacy Emery will hear during debates by presidential candidates is an attack not on a speaker's argument

but instead on that person's character. This fallacy is called **Argumentum Ad Hominem**. It is a version of the fallacy known as **poisoning the well**, for if the source of evidence is discounted, then the evidence from that source becomes impaired in argument. Example: "My opponent speaks sweet words, but let me remind you that he served a prison term for tax fraud."

6. Emery should always be wary when someone tries to appeal to his ego, his vanity, or his insecurities. For example, advertisers will use **counterfeit evidence** in the form of **meaning from association**—they'll try to sell him a car by showing him an actor he likes driving one. Or they'll try **association by continuity** by mentioning in the same breath or in the same sentence two things they want to connect in his mind—a beer they're selling sitting on a table beside priceless old books to suggest that the beer is as finely made as those books. He should be suspicious of "arguments" based on the **prestige of great names**, in other words, an endorsement for a product from famous people, and on **testimonials**. Americans are exposed to over three thousand product messages every day, often with athletes, actors, media celebrities, or doctors who are called upon in advertising to endorse, say, clothing, or whiskey, or anything.

7. But my grandson should think twice when an authority or well-regarded person presents an idea that has nothing to do with his or her field of expertise. This is known as **Misuse of Authority**. A notorious example of this was given to us by William Shockley, an American inventor awarded the 1956 Nobel Prize in Physics, who promoted the most toxic and racist ideas about black people.

8. Another version of the previous fallacy is the **Use of a Confident Manner** by a speaker and the use of **prestige jargon**, that is, technical or foreign languages simply to impress the audience.

9. He should also understand that **repeated assertion** does not count as an argument.

10. When dialoguing with another, Emery and the other person should *define their terms* to make sure they are using the same meaning or definition for what they are discussing. Doing so will avoid **equivocation** or using two meanings for the same word. Emery and his interlocutor should not engage in **pettifogging**, which is making a big deal out of some insignificant aspect of an argument, splitting hairs, or just quibbling to evade

addressing the real issue at hand. If his discussion with another becomes contentious, he would be wise to end the discussion, to pause, step back from it, and determine where it has gone off the rails.

11. Emery should realize that lack of evidence to prove your opponent's position does not prove your own. Making such an assumption is the fallacy known as **Argumentum Ad Ignorantium**.

12. Those in Emery's generation (and our own) should not make assumptions about cause and effect. When we see two things that occur together and close to one another in time (for example, I never have trouble when I carry my lucky rabbit's foot), the wise thing to do is practice skepticism until a relationship is established by undeniable evidence.

13. All in all, then, the general principles for critical thinking that I wish for my grandson to absorb can be summed up in two final bundles of advice. Or really with a single word common to both law and science: evidence. He should always seek verifiable evidence that is complete, and not selective. Examine premises in an argument to make sure they are true (and do not hide their assumptions), and make sure that someone's con-

clusions do not **beg the question** by assuming exactly what one is trying to prove. He should never forget that extraordinary claims require extraordinary evidence.

14. He should avoid being presented with the fallacy of a **false choice** or **either-or dilemma** such as "America, love it or leave it," or "Make love, not war," because other alternates may exist. Those are also examples of the errors in thinking known as **Oversimplification** and the **Black-or-White Fallacy**. He should recognize **contradictory assumptions** when he hears them. ("If elected, I will treat all citizens equally and work for higher taxation of the wealthy.") He should not make assumptions or fall for the trick of **leading questions**. ("Have you stopped beating your spouse yet?") Nor should he alter someone's speech by **lifting it out of context**. I would also caution him against **cliché thinking** (an old saw like "The early bird gets the worm" will have another equally hoary bit of common wisdom that contradicts it) and against the **misuse of analogy**, because while the similarities between two things may be real, they may also be superficial, and we may not have reason for insisting that other similarities exist. Finally, it might help Emery if he remembers that when you *assume* anything, you make an **ASS** out of **U** and **Me**.

It is often said in spiritual literature that speech is the great-grandson of truth. This is, in part, so, because it is quite easy to commit the fallacies in thinking that I've listed above. There are, of course, many more fallacies than the common ones I've described in this chapter. I know I'm sometimes guilty of one or more of these when I'm thinking or speaking carelessly. So I try to remind myself, as I practice mindfulness meditation, to not be so quick to open my mouth until I have interrogated those thoughts and feeling for their accuracy, their logic and veracity, and not until they have stood before the Three Gates.

8

YOU ARE ALREADY PERFECT AND WHOLE, BUT...

I want Emery to understand that he is already whole and perfect, and that nothing needs to be added to his being for him to experience happiness. After all, it takes an entire planet, indeed an entire universe, to support and nourish his being.

But…

While he is whole and perfect as he is, and lacking nothing he needs for happiness, I will counsel him to continually strive to reach beyond his current set of skills, and if only just for the joy that experience of growth will bring to him physically, intellectually, and spiritually. One day I'll ask him to read the daunting and at times humorous list of things that science fiction author Robert Heinlein felt every civilized person should be able to do:

> A human being should be able to change a diaper, plan an invasion, butcher a hog, conn a ship, design a building, write a sonnet, balance accounts, build a wall, set a bone, comfort the dying, take orders, give orders, cooperate, act alone, solve equations, analyze a new problem, pitch manure, program a computer, cook a tasty meal, fight efficiently, die gallantly. Specialization is for insects.

Heinlein's list has twenty-one skills. I'll confess to my grandson that I can only do ten of the things mentioned above, but I can do things his list does not mention. I suspect that being able to "fight efficiently" is one of Heinlein's abilities that I've developed after all the decades I've practiced Asian martial arts, though getting into a fight is the last thing I—and any martial artist—wishes to do, the reason for which I'll explain in this chapter.

It pleases me greatly that Emery began, at age seven, training with a karate club. He just walked into my study with a book he's reading, *Laugh-Out-Loud Jokes for Kids* by Rob Elliott.

"Grandpa," he asks, "how did the karate teacher greet his students?"

I tell him I dunno.

He says, "*Hi*-Yah!" and laughs widely. Then he lays another groaner on me:

"What did the alien say to the plant?"

When I tell him I have no idea, Emery cackles, "Take me to your weeder!"

So, like me, he loves jokes and martial arts. Just the other day, he proudly showed me the blocks, punches, and kicks he's learning. I gave him a few pointers on how to improve his horse-riding stance, break his front thrust kick into four easy moves, and maintain his balance when kicking.

I believe any young (or old) person who is able should engage in some form of daily exercise, for the benefits from doing so are well-documented. But in the case of Asian martial arts, there is more offered here than just "exercise." Those of us who are lifelong practitioners of a martial art usually say we engage in this activity for health and self-defense. But we never—*ever*—start fights. We can end them, though. But only after the most extreme conditions have been met. For example, many of my teachers emphasized that if someone was threatening us with violence, the best tactic is to run. And if we ran into a wall? We were advised to tear down or climb over it. It is only when we or someone we love or care about is cornered that we fight. And then we fight with full commitment, as if our life depended on it, because it probably does.

If we fight, we know the possible consequences of causing serious injury or death to another. The legal problems that can follow a fight—one you *win*—are painful to consider. If you train in the martial arts, the law is stacked against you if you knock someone out or damage them for life. A judge will say, "You have training so why did you use lethal force?" Furthermore, there is the possibility that we may not emerge from a fight unscathed. Any of us might lose an eye or sustain an injury that will haunt us for the rest of our lives.

Unlike what Emery sees in movies and on television, where beautifully choreographed fight scenes go on and on, with flashy high kicks and athletic moves that look good on camera, real fights are over quickly. A three-move combination delivered faster than thought to vulnerable pressure points—those same points you see on acupuncture charts—can bring a confrontation to an end in seconds. So while what he sees on television and in movies may amuse him, he should regard all that as fantasy. Fighting is ugly. It isn't fun. But sometimes in our society—in our world—so drenched in violence, it is necessary to know self-defense.

The importance of dedication to a sport or any physical training—whether that be golf, tennis (or even table tennis), basketball, or soccer, which is the sport I went out for my sophomore year in high school—lies in the emphasis it places on self-control and discipline. But it's martial arts that I'm most familiar with, and how in the *dōjō* or *kwoon*, classes may end with sitting meditation. Emery will learn respect for an opponent when he steps out on the deck to face him or her. Who he is—his level of attainment in the school—will be symbolized by the color of the belt he wears around the waist of his white gi. It won't matter if he is rich or poor, black or white, male or female. It won't matter who his parents or grandparents are, or what his family history is, or whether he's a janitor or a college professor, or what his degrees are, or how many books he's published, or languages he's learned, or whether his ancestors were masters or slaves. He can bring *none* of that onto the deck (or into a boxing ring or a tennis court) when he is sparring right *here*, right *now*—he steps in that space only with what he has earned through nights of sweat, conditioning, and ever pushing beyond what he believed his physical and spiritual limits might be.

One day I'll tell Emery about the worst martial art

student I've ever seen. This was in the late 1960s. I was an undergraduate, working out with a karate club that met on the campus I attended. The rest of us were all ego-filled young bucks dying to spar, to show off what we could do—flying side kicks, flurry punches, spin-around back kicks, foot sweeps. I don't recall this student's name, but no one wanted to spar with him because he was so inept and slow and lacking in confidence. He was small and slight of build. Everybody whupped on him. He'd probably been bullied all his life—in elementary, middle, and high school—and he was in class with us because he hoped to change that. Naturally, one Saturday afternoon he was paired up with me. Grudgingly, I went out on the deck and bowed to him, but I was thinking to myself, *This guy can't fight. What can I do to keep myself from being bored?* Suddenly an idea came to me. As he hesitantly and awkwardly came toward me, I threw a low front snap kick to force him to instinctively tilt forward as he tried a downward block, then I let my kick swing suddenly around in an arc, which smacked him—*whack!*—loudly right in his face. The sound of it filled the room. He was shocked and bewildered. The class erupted. I mean, the other students went crazy. There was no kick like that in this system. Our teacher ran up to me and said, "What was *that*?" I told him I didn't know; I'd just made it up.

What I learned later in another school was that I'd
just thrown a simple inside crescent kick—before I knew
what one was. Of course, the student I kicked endured
humiliation. Every class was a defeat for him. But he
never missed class. As the academic quarter wore on, I
watched him absorb more punishment from the other students. More humiliation. He *really* wanted to learn and
wouldn't quit, regardless of what the cost to his ego—and
the punishment to his body—might be. And slowly, like
the proverbial tortoise, his stances improved. As did all
his techniques. I watched the slow-as-molasses-in-winter
changes take place, and a profound respect for him dawned
in me. And admiration. He was not a natural athlete. And
so he had absorbed punishment like the rest of us never
knew—*from* us, but in the end he emerged, as if from a
chrysalis, more confident, more skillful, and more sure
of himself precisely because he had overcome so much
pain, humiliation, and fear to attain what came easily for
the rest of us. Yeah, I'll one day tell my grandson, that
young man earned respect from all of us the hard way.
He was a fighter in spirit. He represented the best martial
arts training had to offer.

Just as the practice of meditation is not confined to
one's cushion (zafu), Emery will come to understand
that his life itself is the practice. He will always be aware
of his body among other bodies in the world. He will

know how to breathe when moving, and how to make his movements as economical, efficient, and graceful as those of a fish in water, or a bird riding the wind. Wherever he goes, whatever room he walks into, he enters as someone alert, aware of where he is at every moment, and of others around him—and of what he has attained from training. From being tested. He will feel relaxed in his mind and body wherever he is. The very way he will carry himself, the way he walks, will discourage hostility from others. Everything he does in his school or away from it, should involve *spirit first, technique second*. (I daresay that principle also applies to writing and drawing and any of the arts.)

If the confidence he gains from martial arts training troubles people who are less confident, I'll simply ask him to recall something once said by actor Bette Davis: "I was thought to be 'stuck up.' I wasn't. I was just sure of myself. This is and always has been an unforgivable quality to the unsure."

And my grandson should not worry overly much about how much progress he is making toward his first black belt. To help him, I'll tell him a story about an overly eager student of Zen:

A young and eager student came to his teacher one day, and asked the Master, "If I work very hard and diligently, how long will it take for me to find Zen?" The Master thought about this, and said, "Ten years…" The student then said, "But what if I work very, very hard and really apply myself to learn fast. How long then?" The Master said, "Well, in that case, it will take twenty years."

"But," said the student, "if I really, really work at it, how long then?" The Master considered this, and said, "Thirty years." Now the increasingly frustrated student wailed, "I don't understand! Whenever I say I will work harder, you tell me it's going to take me longer. Why do you say that?" After a moment, the Master said, "When you have one eye on the goal, you only have one eye on the path."

Put another way, it is the journey to excellence that will enrich him, not the belt at the end of the road. And that first-degree is just a beginning for more degrees that await him, if he wishes to continue beyond that first big benchmark or milestone.

What if Emery finally attains his first-degree black belt after years of patient training? After a grueling black-belt test—breaking wood or bricks with his hand, sparring against multiple opponents, performing a kata that he has created—that will leave him fatigued in every fiber, but also filled with pride and humility? It is said that only one of a thousand students who begins training in karate will reach the first black-belt level. What will he feel? I think he will realize that he is still a beginner, hopefully one with the Beginner's Mind of Zen, a mind and spirit always fresh and open, not fixed or frozen, always flowing like water. Emery will see that his learning through karate has no end.

In his classic work, *Karate-Dō: My Way of Life*, master martial artist Gichin Funakoshi explained that "any place can be a *dōjō*," and that seeing karate as being only about fighting is a mistake. For a long time I've loved Funakoshi's memoir for its earned wisdom, such as "What you have been taught by listening to others' words you will forget very quickly; what you have learned with your whole body you will remember for the rest of your life."

When Emery sees me leaving on Wednesday nights to work out with old friends in their fifties and sixties (I'm the oldest member of a group of Choy Li Fut practitioners), he always asks if he can come along. One night, a year or so ago, I did take him to class. We devoted the entire night to him, showing him how to practice his kicks and punches on a focus mitt. His techniques were surprisingly strong, but at the end of a couple of hours he did seem a little tired.

I imagined he saw how much fun it is for me to work out with old friends. Some days one may feel too tired to work out on one's own. However, if friends are waiting for me, I know I simply must be there. That I shouldn't let them down or bail out for the evening unless I have a very good reason for doing so. In class, we review our old sets, practice drills, teach each other new sets in our system, and, of course, we socialize—tell jokes, tease each other, and catch up on our personal lives as we work up a good sweat. All in all, such weekly practice is, as Funakoshi tells us, "above all else, a faith, a way of life."

9

NEVER STOP LEARNING

It is our duty to be discontented with the measure we have of knowledge & virtue, to forget the things behind & press toward those before.

Ralph Waldo Emerson

If Emery hasn't lost patience or become bored by my advice in the earlier chapters, he probably has begun to detect a leitmotif in what I've been telling him. Namely, that I want him to be a lifelong learner. He will need to understand, of course, the importance of epistemological humility, that is, to see in a universe as vast and mysterious as ours that our knowledge is necessarily always incomplete, partial, and provisional, and that our opinions are merely that—just limited views shaped by our conditioning in the social world.

With that caveat said, I can tick off on my fingers the well-known rewards that come from being a lifelong learner. Greater earning power is obviously one such reward. But there is another benefit that I'd like to highlight based on a recent article by Anne Tergesen titled "What Science Tells Us about Preventing Dementia." It states that there are no guarantees for preventing dementia as we age, but there are things we all can do to reduce the risk of developing Alzheimer's later in life. "It's a package of behaviors," Sarah Lenz Lock, executive director of AARP's Global Council on Brain Health, states in this article, "including aerobic exercise, strength training, a healthy diet, sleep and cognitive training." The article then says, "Because most neurodegenerative diseases take years, if not decades, to develop, researchers say the best time to focus on brain health is long before symptoms occur—ideally by midlife if not before. Still, they emphasize that it is never too late to start."

I think eight-year-old Emery is already on the right lifestyle path with his physical training so it's his cognitive training that I feel I should talk about. "Many population studies," reports this article on Alzheimer's, "suggest that education increases cognitive reserve, a term for the brain's ability to compensate for neurological damage." Furthermore, one reliable study found that "people who engaged in more than six activities a month—including hobbies, reading, visiting friends, walking, volunteering and attending religious services—had a 38 percent lower rate of developing dementia than people who did fewer activities."

If Emery asks me what hobby or activity I recommend for improving cognitive reserve, I won't hesitate to say his study of a foreign language, even though I, his grandfather, have never had any natural talent for learning a second or third language. They don't come easily to me, probably because as the visual artist I've been since childhood I'm more oriented toward what I see rather than what I hear. (Or at least that's my rationalization.) Sure, I'll tell my grandson, I dutifully studied Spanish for seven years from middle school through undergraduate college, then I did a year of French (reading only, not speaking) as the language requirement for my master's degree in philosophy. But I had to work at that study. I struggled with it, knowing that if I didn't invest at least an hour a day I'd forget what I learned.

But all that changed in 1998.

When I received a MacArthur Fellowship that year, my present to myself, at age fifty, was the systematic and sustained study of Sanskrit, a language that had fascinated me since the late 1960s. Perhaps I changed because Sanskrit ignited my passion. My entry point was provided by the very effective approach utilized by the American Sanskrit Institute, an approach that united mind, body, and spirit. My teacher was (is) Aja Thomas, a Vedic priest who operates the Atma Institute in Portland, Oregon. For many years, Aja drove up from Portland to offer two or three days of immersion in Sanskrit to our Seattle study group, which translated large portions of the *Bhagavad Gita*, *Yoga Sutras of Patanjali*, the *Astavakra Samhita*, and other texts.

The approach we were taught was holistic—one has to give up limited concerns of self to make progress. We do not study for grades or degrees, only because we love the beauty of this language and the role it has played for roughly four thousand years in influencing cultures Western and Eastern. Aja would write a verse on the board and before we translated it, everyone in our group (I was almost always the only male, the others being women who taught yoga) had to sing it individually, which was something I had to work up the courage to do in front of others—I'm no Marvin Gaye. After that, we worked on vocabulary and grammar, and later we discussed the verse's meaning before singing it again as a group. This process typically took about two or three hours and required our complete attention.

In other words, the approach amounted to focused meditation, with the emphasis being on experiencing maximum, interrupted resonance, perfectly blended syllables for the joy they bring, and recognizing visual symbols: *speech as music*. That is somewhat different from the more academic approach one finds at universities, which emphasizes memorization and a competitive "success/failure" model that detotalizes the learning experience. (According to Sanskrit teacher Vyaas Houston, "At our highest centers of learning, the best universities, the dropout rate for Sanskrit classes can be as high as 90 percent.")

Over the decades, I've developed a pretty extensive library on this language and its children, because Sanskrit shares much in common not only with the Celtic, Teutonic, Slavonic, Germanic, and Anglo-Saxon languages but also Asian ones such as Pali, Hindi, Marathi, and Gandhari. The oldest Buddhist manuscripts we have on fragile and brittle two-thousand-year-old fragments of birch bark are in Gandhari, a dialect of Prakrit, which developed from Sanskrit; they were found in a jar in a cave in eastern Afghanistan, were written when Jesus was still alive, and are being translated by my colleague Richard Salomon and his team in the Department of Asian Languages and Literature at the University of Washington; see his 1999 work, with an introduction by the Dalai Lama, entitled *Ancient Buddhist Scrolls from Gandhara: The British Library Kharosthi Fragments.*

It seems to me that, as Emerson once said, "Language is the archive of history." To learn another language, then, is to learn human histories other than one's own. Furthermore, it is to experience the world differently as it is lensed through a foreign language. Some words—or experiences—have no exact equivalent in English. One I love is the Thai word "riabroi," which means "Everything together at once, complete, sensible, beautiful, perfect, and natural." I heard it used by a flight attendant during a research trip to Thailand in 1997 when my two guides and I were returning to Chiang Mai from time spent with the Hmong hill tribesmen near the Laos border. She used it to assure us passengers that we had landed safely—but *more* than just safely.

Emery has probably heard me end my meditation sessions by softly chanting Sanskrit mantras or lines I've memorized from texts that I love. Each line of Sanskrit is compressed, much like in an equation, math, or calculus. The word "Sanskrit" (*Sanskrta*) itself means "language brought to formal perfection." (NASA discovered in its early AI research that Sanskrit is the only unambiguous language on Earth.) As Vyaas Houston put it, "the extraordinary thing about Sanskrit is that it offers direct accessibility by anyone to that elevated plane where the two, mathematics and music, brain and heart, analytic and intuitive, scientific and spiritual become one."

Its rewards seem endless. It is the language of mantras. It is the language of enlightenment, and it requires the one-pointedness (*ekagratha* or "single-grasping") of yoga. It demands a different way of seeing and experiencing the world. When he was jailed by the British, Gandhi studied Sanskrit and the *Gita*. Writing in Devanagari is like drawing or doing calligraphy. The Buddhist texts I once studied in different translations, like the *Dhammapada* and *Prajna-Paramita-Hridaya-Sutra*, I have now translated myself, an exercise that reinforces the old truth that any translation from a foreign language (especially a "dead" one) can yield multiple interpretations. Speaking and reading Sanskrit, we find ourselves sensitized to the sound (guttural, palatal, cerebral, dental, and labial) and the music of language, so much so that when I was still teaching and turned to going over the English prose of my students after a Sanskrit study session (and playfully slipped into translating their sentences into Sanskrit as I do sometimes when reading news stories), I found my ear more finely tuned to each syllable. For example, the word *upadēsha* means "instruction." More specifically, *upa* means "near," and *dēsha* means "pointing." Instruction, therefore, is "pointing near." In other words, when instructing others, we can only point at the subject, never deliver it.

My grandson Emery will see that Sanskrit is my most

serious intellectual and spiritual hobby, a language I will study until the last day of my life, especially because so many studies show that for older people language study keeps their minds sharp. But I will never consider myself to be an "expert," only and always an avid learner.

10

TO LOVE IS
TO LIVE

I could go on and on, sharing with Emery his grandfather's experiences as he circled the sun seventy-two times. What I learned from working blue-collar jobs in my youth beside unpretentious, older men whose life circumstances would keep them on those jobs long after I left to return to college. And what I learned, as a cartoonist during my undergraduate days, from men who were incarcerated. My PBS series, *Charlie's Pad*, was on the air in 1970, and inmates would write to me about the dreams they hoped to realize when they were released. I don't remember who invited me, but I could tell my grandson that I drove to Marion Prison in southern Illinois, the highest maximum-security prison in America, built to replace Alcatraz. I will never forget that evening—the series of metal doors that locked with a clang behind me as I made my way inside, and the way the young, black prisoners came through a tunnel-like corridor (so low they had to walk stooped over) to the conference room where I was waiting to meet them with my drawing pad and a black marker. I gave them what cartoonists call a "chalk talk," that is, I gave them a few drawing lessons. They asked me to draw pretty women for them, which I did.

And decades later in Seattle, I'd say to my grandson that in my role as a writer I went to a lockup facility for offenders under the age of eighteen who were awaiting trial. All the kids wore different colored jumpsuits and soft slippers. I remember one young man who approached me before my talk to say that he read I'd kept a diary as a kid. He told me that inspired him to do the same during his time behind bars so that one day his baby son could read it and not make the same mistakes he did.

If he cares to listen, I can tell Emery what it's like to support a family from a young age, simultaneously looking backward to take care of the needs of one's own

aging parents, and forward to emotionally and finan-
cially supporting a spouse, then a son and daughter from
K-12 through their college years, doing one's best to prepare them to pursue *their* dreams—"having their back,"
as the saying goes—every day when they feel blue, or
when another adult treats them unfairly and they need
a strong parent to make a way for them in the less than
coherent world that other grown-ups have created. For
me, having a child—a being completely helpless and dependent on me for its survival—meant that when I was
in my twenties I had to stop being a child myself. I can
tell him my takeaway from parenthood is that it never
really ends, that it's a lifetime sentence one generally
serves happily and to the best of one's ability, using that
special relationship between parent and child as a daily
opportunity to reduce—as a caregiver—one's own self-
will and selfishness for the sake of loved ones.

I could hip Emery to the long odyssey involved in earning academic degrees that led to professorship, and what
the challenges were like at a school where only 2 percent
of the faculty were black. There, I'll tell him, if he goes
into higher education—what Saul Bellow in *Humboldt's
Gift* called "the academic music box"—he'll find the full
range of human personality types—the dull and geniuses,
the emotionally mature and the childish, the egocentric and
the unselfish, the unoriginal and the brilliant, the lazy and

the hardworking, the neurotically depressed and the spiritually centered. Among these will be supportive coworkers and even the workplace bully jealous of any advancements in salary and rank others might achieve—people with a sadly zero-sum way of thinking, who have yet to learn that just because the rain and sunshine cause one flower to bloom, it doesn't mean other flowers won't bloom, as well.

I want my grandson's life to circle the sun more times than I've made on my journey so far. If that happens, I imagine that he will be washed by all waters. And I want him to see that what is most important, regardless of the social or economic circumstances in which he finds himself, is the intention that he brings to whatever he does. Saint Catherine of Genoa's advice might help him stay the course if he remembers, "We must not wish anything other than what happens from moment to moment, all the while, however, exercising ourselves in goodness."

One day I guess I'll have to talk with him about romance, and the intricacies of love between friends (*philias*), between people just hot to trot (*eros*), and the unconditional, teleological love called *agape*, where one loves the potential one sees in another, as every good parent loves his or her child. I will tell him, candidly, that during my life's journey, his grandfather was blessed to experience all three forms of the love just mentioned (and more). My deepest wish is that he will find a part-

ner or companion who is a creative, smart, compassion-
ate, resourceful, and very giving person. I will hope
that the love they share never fades, feels as natural as a
force of nature, as something mandated by their karma,
with neither of them bringing any baggage or negativity to the relationship. With trust and transparency, I
would hope they can be vulnerable together, accepting each other just as they are, completely giving all of
themselves—in mind, body, and spirit—to the other. I
would hope that Emery and his companion will be able
to open reservoirs of love in one another. With this kind
of love, they will make each other better, walking hand
in hand through a society, a world, where love so often
seems in short supply. Such a love will fill them with
thanksgiving, deepen their sense of wonder, and awaken
a fearlessness in their heart. May my grandson, and all
the children of his generation, someday experience such
a nonexploitative love that humbles two people with its
beauty and deepens their humanity. I want them to understand that there is no greater experience that we can
have than love, for that is the wellspring from which all
good things flow.

I'm writing this chapter in the wee hours of morning,
at 4:30 a.m., because I keep the same night-owl hours as
Descartes, Balzac, and Langston Hughes. Everyone in

my house is supposed to be sleeping, but into my study rushes Emery, startling me.

"I need a flashlight," he announces.

For a moment I just stare, wondering how come this kid is awake before daylight.

"Why?"

"Because," he says, "I had a dream, and a creepy person was chasing me."

"Why was he creepy?"

"He was wearing underwear on his head."

I concede, yes, that's creepy, but then I wonder, "Why do you need the flashlight?"

"To scare him off, Grandpa."

"Uh…okay."

He goes right to the corner of the room where I keep a few small penlights, grabs one, and hurries out. He knew exactly where they were, of course. Since this cluttered study has become as much his workplace as mine.

★ ★ ★ ★ ★

ACKNOWLEDGMENTS

First, I would like to thank the publishers of *3rd Act* magazine for publishing the essay "Advice to Emery," which was the basis for this book. Very special thanks are due to my superb editor, John Glynn, for making this book possible, and for his careful editing. I would also like to thank Brian McDonald for giving me permission to include his real-life story; philosopher Michael Boylan for his assistance with the chapter explaining logical fallacies; my agent for speaking engagements, Jodi Solomon, for her unwavering support; writer Sharyn Skeeter for her helpful editorial corrections and suggestions as I worked through the manuscript; and my literary agents, Georges and Anne Borchardt, for the forty-seven years they have represented my work and helped me navigate the literary world.